AGAINST ALL ODDS

HOW THE OHIO STATE BUCKEYES WON THEIR
8TH NATIONAL CHAMPIONSHIP

LANTERN EDITORS:

Editor-in-Chief	Liz Young
Managing Editor, Content	Michele Theodore
Managing Editor, Design	Madison Curtis
Copy Chief	Grant Miller
Sports Editor	Tim Moody
Asst. Sports Editor	James Grega
Arts Editor	Danielle Seamon
Asst. Arts Editor	Daniel Bendtsen
Campus Editor	Logan Hickman
Photo Editor	Mark Batke
Asst. Photo Editor	Jon McAllister
Multimedia Editor	Chelsea Spears
Asst. Multimedia Editor	Hannah Chenetski
Asst. Multimedia Editor	Khalid Moalim
Design Editor	Kelsey Wagner
Design Editor	Eileen McClory
Oller Reporter	Alex Drummer

LANTERN TV STAFF:

Station Manager	Franz Ross
News Director	Ritika Shah
Asst. News Director	Ariana Bernard
Sports Director	Hayden Grove
Asst. Sports Director	Aaron Yerian

STAFF

Faculty Advisers	Dan Caterinicchia
	Nicole Kraft
Advertising	Aaron Bass
General Manager	Rick Szabrak
Production/Webmaster	Jay Smith
Lantern TV Production	Tao Wang

Peter J. Clark, Publisher
Molly Voorheis, Managing Editor
Nicky Brillowski, Book and Cover Design
Kitty Grigsby, Layout
Sam Schmidt, Advertising

ISBN: 978-1-940056-16-6

Printed in the United States of America
KCI Sports Publishing   3340 Whiting Avenue, Suite 5   Stevens Point, WI 54481
Phone: 1-800-697-3756   Fax: 715-344-2668
www.kcisports.com

CONTENTS

Head coach Urban Meyer hands the national championsip trophy to running back Ezekiel Elliott following the Buckeyes win over the Oregon Ducks in the College Football Playoff National Championship at AT&T Stadium in Arlington, TX. *Ray Carlin | AP Photo*

OHIO STATE BUCKEYES

NCAA NATIONAL CHAMPIONS

OHIO STATE FOOTBALL GOALS UNCHANGED AFTER BRAXTON MILLER'S INJURY

by Tim Moody

In the Ohio State football team meeting room, a sign details the Buckeyes' "plan to win." The plan lists playing great defense first, followed by winning the turnover battle, scoring in the red zone and winning the kicking game.

That plan was designed to put the Buckeyes in a position to win Big Ten and national titles, and that doesn't have to change after senior quarterback Braxton Miller suffered a season-ending injury Monday.

OSU coach Urban Meyer said Miller's injury — which he said is a torn labrum in the signal caller's throwing shoulder — caused a "devastating" moment on the practice field. However, the team has come back strong since then, he added.

"Really impressed," the third-year OSU coach said. "The energy, the speed; I think they see the light at the end of the tunnel, so it was a very, very good day of practice."

Meyer said moving forward without Miller is a "huge test" for his team, but the players have been up to the challenge so far.

While Miller did account for 44 percent of OSU's offense last season, Meyer said the most important thing right now is getting his team ready — no matter who is on the field. He said a quarterback is an "important cog" in the team, but there is more than that to winning football games.

"One thing our team is pretty good at, and I've gotten better at, is worrying about the moment," Meyer said. "And the moment is getting a team ready."

Senior wide receiver Evan Spencer said there will be changes to the offense, but agreed that

J.T. BARRETT

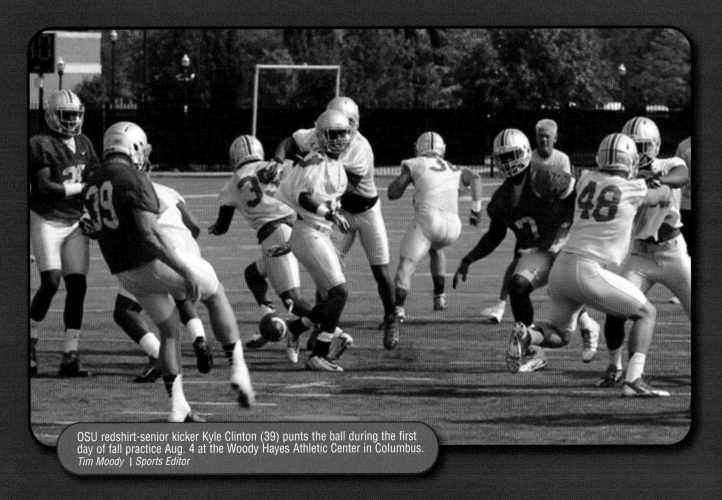

OSU redshirt-senior kicker Kyle Clinton (39) punts the ball during the first day of fall practice Aug. 4 at the Woody Hayes Athletic Center in Columbus.
Tim Moody | *Sports Editor*

redshirt-freshman quarterback J.T. Barrett, as well as Cardale Jones if he plays any reps, will be ready to go because of the amount of practice time they've had since the season ended.

"They've been throwing the ball so much all throughout camp, and really all throughout the offseason, that it's not that much of a transition for us just because that's what we've been going through," Spencer said.

While many wrote off OSU as a contender in the National Championship race after Miller went down, Spencer said he's seen enough in practice to have plenty of confidence heading into the season.

"Personally, I think what we've been seeing out at practice — and a lot of the other seniors can back me up — is ... we'll be way more than all right this year," he said. "That's for sure."

While Barrett has been penciled in to Miller's previously set-in-stone spot, players on the defensive side of the ball know they have to step up just as much as the offense.

"Play great defense" is No. 1 on OSU's plan to win, after all.

Senior linebacker Curtis Grant, who is entering his second season as a starter on the Buckeye defense, said the injury to Miller doesn't have to mean more pressure for the defense.

He said that adding pressure on oneself can lead to a decreased quality of play on the field. At the end of the day, Curtis Grant said the Buckeye defense just has to keep doing what they always do.

"We still go out there and have fun and play the game," he said. "Because that's what we're here for."

In 2013, the Buckeye defense gave up 5,284 yards of total offense, including 3,752 yards through the air. Those numbers, especially coming on the heels of two consecutive losses to the end the season, are considered subpar by some for the famed Silver Bullets defense.

"I mean, we have to take it to another level just coming back from last season," senior cornerback Doran Grant said of the team's defensive outlook this fall. "That's just something we have to do."

Playing great defense is certainly still in the plans for OSU, as are winning the turnover battle, scoring in the red zone and winning the kicking game.

Things will certainly be different for OSU in a full season without Miller, but the Buckeyes don't think that has to change their ceiling in 2014.∎

BUCKEYES 34
MIDSHIPMEN 17

OSU redshirt-freshman quarterback J.T. Barrett warms up before a game against Navy. *Mark Batke* | *Photo Editor*

REDSHIRT FRESHMEN LEAD OHIO STATE OVER NAVY

U.S. Naval Academy students march on the field prior to kickoff to help sing the national anthem. *Mark Batke* | *Photo Editor*

by Tim Moody

In the first game since senior quarterback Braxton Miller was ruled out for the season, two redshirt-freshmen boosted the Ohio State football team to a 34-17 win against Navy.

After a low-scoring first half that saw the Midshipmen take a 7-6 lead, redshirt-freshman linebacker Darron Lee and redshirt-freshman quarterback J.T. Barrett each accounted for second-half touchdowns in the team's season opener Saturday at M&T Bank Stadium.

Lee picked up a Navy fumble early in the third quarter and took it 61 yards for a score to give

OHIO STATE BUCKEYES

the Buckeyes their first lead of the day, 13-7.

OSU coach Urban Meyer said he believed Lee's touchdown was a key to the Buckeyes eventually coming out on top, along with multiple defensive stands throughout the day.

"The turning point was, I think, the Darron Lee fumble return," Meyer said after the game. "That and the fact that our defense kept everything in check — even when I went for it on fourth down and we did not get it."

"When I was an assistant coach at Notre Dame, that was always the worst week of the year, every time that we had to prepare for Navy," Meyer said. "The best thing about today was that it's in the rearview mirror and we won."

Barrett, who became the Buckeyes' starter when Miller tore his labrum in fall camp, gave OSU a 20-14 lead with an 80-yard touchdown pass to senior wide receiver Devin Smith in the third quarter.

"They bit so hard on the play action, I was just trying not to miss him," Barrett said after the game. "He made a great catch and then just ran away from (the defense)."

OSU redshirt-sophomore wide receiver Michael Thomas scores a touchdown against Navy.
Mark Batke | *Photo Editor*

NCAA NATIONAL CHAMPIONS

OSU freshman running back Curtis Samuel (4) rushes the ball past Navy players. *Mark Batke* | *Photo Editor*

The downfield strike came after Barrett had a slow start to the game, marked by a first half interception thrown in the red zone that ended a promising drive.

"After the interception, I was like: 'J.T., you knew you shouldn't have thrown it, you shouldn't have thrown it, now you got to make up for it,'" Meyer said.

Despite the mistake, Meyer said Barrett kept a level head throughout the game and added that he expects the Wichita Falls, Texas, native to improve throughout the season.

"His demeanor was great, he's a great kid," Meyer said. "He'll get better and better and better."

After the Smith touchdown, Navy tacked on a field goal with 13:54 to play to make it 20-17 before OSU sophomore running back Ezekiel Elliott scampered in for a touchdown from 10 yards out on the Buckeyes' next drive. That drive included a fourth-and-short conversion by Elliott. Navy coach Ken Niumatalolo challenged the spot of the ball, but the call stood to extend the drive.

The challenge ended up costing Navy its final timeout of the game.

Niumatalolo said the Midshipmen had "no choice" but to challenge the play, despite the potential consequences.

"It's hard because our guys have invested so

much," he said. "These guys have worked their butts off for eight months, and everything we've done this offseason pointed to this game."

After the failed challenge and Elliott's touchdown, the Midshipmen got the ball back with a little over eight minutes left and needing a touchdown.

While Navy had success running the ball for much of the game — they had 370 rushing yards on the day — the OSU defense rose to the occasion and forced another punt. Barrett promptly led the Buckeyes back down the field and found redshirt-sophomore wide receiver Michael Thomas for a nine-yard touchdown. The score proved to be the last of the game, cementing a 17-point Buckeye victory.

Barrett finished the game 12 of 15 passing for 226 yards and a pair of scores with one first-half interception. He also carried the ball nine times for 50 yards, including a key first-down run on third and 11 in the fourth quarter.

Meyer gave Barrett a "B" grade after the game and said he "did okay."

"Every new player will have their mistakes," he said. "We wanted to open it up more in the first half but didn't, and that wasn't because of him. Our offensive line had some mistakes in there with penalties and sacks. We just can't do that up front."∎

OSU players sing 'Carmen Ohio' following a 34-17 win against Navy.
Mark Batke | Photo Editor

BOX SCORE

	1	2	3	4	T
Ohio State #5	3	3	14	14	34
Navy	0	7	7	3	17

SCORING SUMMARY

FIRST QUARTER
OSU FG 4:26 Sean Nuernberger 46 Yd Field Goal
Drive info: 8 plays, 28 yds in 4:25

SECOND QUARTER
NAVY TD 14:04 DeBrandon Sanders 1 Yd Run (Nick Sloan Kick)
Drive info: 11 plays, 75 yds in 5:22
OSU FG 2:04 Sean Nuernberger 28 Yd Field Goal
Drive info: 8 plays, 30 yds in 3:58

THIRD QUARTER
OSU TD 13:08 Darron Lee 61 Yd Fumble Return (Sean Nuernberger Kick)
Drive info: 5 plays, 39 yds in 1:52
NAVY TD 11:15 Keenan Reynolds 1 Yd Run (Nick Sloan Kick)
Drive info: 4 plays, 84 yds in 1:53
OSU TD 4:10 Devin Smith 80 Yd pass from J.T. Barrett (Sean Nuernberger Kick)
Drive info: 1 plays, 80 yds in 0:11

FOURTH QUARTER
NAVY FG 13:54 Nick Sloan 32 Yd Field Goal
Drive info: 11 plays, 61 yds in 5:16
OSU TD 8:54 Ezekiel Elliott 10 Yd Run (Sean Nuernberger Kick)
Drive info: 10 plays, 80 yds in 5:00
OSU TD 2:09 Michael Thomas 9 Yd pass from J.T. Barrett (Sean Nuernberger Kick)
Drive info: 8 plays, 70 yds in 4:48

HOKIES 35
BUCKEYES 21

Ohio State emerged for the first time from the new players tunnel looking ready for battle against Virginia Tech, but the Hokies got the better of the Buckeyes on their home field. *Mark Batke | Photo Editor*

OHIO STATE LOSES FIRST HOME OPENER IN 36 YEARS

Redshirt-freshman linebacker Darron Lee (43) celebrates after making a tackle. *Mark Batke | Photo Editor*

by Tim Moody

In front of a record crowd at Ohio Stadium, the Ohio State football team lost its first home opener since 1978.

OSU fell to Virginia Tech, 35-21, in front of 107,517 at the Horseshoe. The game marked the first regular-season loss for the Buckeyes since coach Urban Meyer took over before the 2012 season.

After the game, Meyer thanked the Ohio Stadium crowd and had praise for Virginia Tech.

"Our opponent really did a good job preparing for us and exposed us a little bit, where some of

J.T. Barrett (16) sheds a tackle from Virginia Tech redshirt-senior linebacker Chase Williams (36) on his way into the end zone.
Mark Batke | Photo Editor

the weaknesses right now on our team are," he said. "And it was rather obvious what it is."

The Hokies had a 14-point lead at halftime and took the lead for good with a touchdown with 8:44 remaining on the clock. OSU redshirt-freshman quarterback J.T. Barrett was sacked six times in the second half on top of throwing three interceptions after the break.

OSU had one last chance to tie the game with a drive that started at its own 29-yard line.

Barrett picked up 22 yards on third and 19 before moving the ball past the 50. A sack made it third and 16 for the Buckeyes before Barrett threw his third interception of the game. Virginia Tech junior cornerback Donovan Riley took the turnover back for a touchdown for the final score of the game.

The touchdown marked the game's final points after OSU had stormed back to threaten Virginia Tech after the early deficit.

Trailing 21-7 and struggling to move the ball in the second half, the Buckeyes ran consecutive options to freshman running back Curtis Samuel resulting in two first downs. Two plays later, Barrett hit redshirt-sophomore wide receiver Michael Thomas for a 53-yard touchdown, bringing

OSU back within seven.

Sophomore safety Vonn Bell intercepted Virginia Tech redshirt-junior quarterback Michael Brewer on the ensuing drive to give OSU the ball inside the 50.

OSU's drive stalled, but sophomore punter Cameron Johnston pinned the Hokies inside the 10-yard line.

On second down with 12 yards to go, sophomore defensive lineman Joey Bosa sacked Brewer and forced a fumble to give the Buckeyes the ball in the red zone.

OSU took just 12 seconds to score on the next drive when sophomore running back Ezekiel Elliott scampered in from 15 yards out to tie the game at 21.

Redshirt-senior kicker Kyle Clinton booted the kickoff out of bounds to give the Hokies a short field. Brewer capitalized with a 10-yard touchdown pass to put Virginia Tech back on top, 28-21.

Barrett finished the game nine of 29 on pass attempts for 219 yards and one touchdown. He carried the ball 24 times for 70 yards, hindered by seven sacks. Elliott finished second on the team with 33 rushing yards and a touchdown while Thomas led all receivers in the game with 98 yards on six catches.■

Not even singing 'Carmen Ohio' could lift the spirits of the Ohio State players after the team's shocking loss to Virginia Tech. *Mark Batke | Photo Editor*

BOX SCORE

	1	2	3	4	T
Virginia Tech	14	7	0	14	35
Ohio State #8	7	0	7	7	21

SCORING SUMMARY

FIRST QUARTER

VT   TD   7:05   Shai McKenzie 2 Yd Run (Joey Slye Kick)

Drive info: 10 plays, 43 yds in 4:50

OSU   TD   3:51   J.T. Barrett 2 Yd Run (Sean Nuernberger Kick)

Drive info: 7 plays, 83 yds in 3:14

VT   TD   0:19   Marshawn Williams 14 Yd Run (Joey Slye Kick)

Drive info: 9 plays, 58 yds in 3:32

SECOND QUARTER

VT   TD   0:52   Sam Rogers 10 Yd pass from Michael Brewer (Joey Slye Kick)

Drive info: 8 plays, 61 yds in 1:09

THIRD QUARTER

OSU   TD   3:01   Michael Thomas 53 Yd pass from J.T. Barrett (Sean Nuernberger Kick)

Drive info: 6 plays, 86 yds in 2:26

FOURTH QUARTER

OSU   TD   11:40   Ezekiel Elliott 15 Yd Run (Sean Nuernberger Kick)

Drive info: 2 plays, 15 yds in 0:12

VT   TD   8:44   Bucky Hodges 10 Yd pass from Michael Brewer (Joey Slye Kick)

Drive info: 6 plays, 65 yds in 2:56

VT   TD   0:46   Donovan Riley 63 Yd Interception Return (Joey Slye Kick)

BUCKEYES 66
GOLDEN FLASHES 0

J.T. Barrett dominated Kent State on the ground and in the air, passing for six touchdowns. *Mark Batke | Photo Editor*

OHIO STATE REBOUNDS FROM LOSS, TROUNCES KENT STATE

Curtis Samuel was just one of many countless running threats for the Buckeyes, who took the lead early and never looked back.
Mark Batke | Photo Editor

by Tim Moody

One week removed from its first loss of the season, the Ohio State football team jumped out to a 21-0 first-quarter lead on its way to beating Kent State, 66-0.

The Buckeyes scored less than two minutes into the game to start things off before scoring touchdowns on six of eight first-half drives Saturday at Ohio Stadium.

NCAA NATIONAL CHAMPIONS

OSU coach Urban Meyer credited the win partially to the Buckeyes' advantage in the talent column, and added his team needed a big game coming off a 35-21 loss to Virginia Tech on September 6.

"I thought our guys played well," Meyer said after the win. "Obviously a little talent advantage, but we had to have a game like this."

Redshirt-freshman quarterback J.T. Barrett tied an OSU record with six touchdown passes in the game — five of which came in the first half.

The Wichita Falls, Texas, native attempted 19 passes in the first quarter alone as Meyer said throwing the ball early and often was a big part of the Buckeyes' game plan.

"Early in the first half I wanted to throw a lot," Meyer said after

Sophomore running back Ezekiel Elliott (15) proves a force to be reckoned with, as he runs the ball against Kent State. *Mark Batke | Photo Editor*

OSU redshirt-junior tight end Nick Vannett (81) carries the ball. *Mark Batke | Photo Editor*

the game. "I wanted to force him (Barrett) to make plays, and the receivers — it's not just him, it's the whole combination of quarterback/receivers."

OSU tacked on 21 points in the second half to close out the scoring and improve its record to 2-1 on the season.

Three different Buckeyes scored the first touchdowns of their college careers as role players saw time in both halves for OSU.

Redshirt-freshman tight end Marcus Baugh scored a touchdown in the first half on the first reception of his college career. In the second half, redshirt-freshman H-back Jalin Marshall and freshman running back Curtis Samuel each made it into the end zone for the first time in their OSU careers as well.

"I had a smile from my ear to ear," Marshall said of his first touchdown with the Scarlet and Gray. "And it felt really good."

Barrett totaled 297 passing yards in the first half alone before tacking on 15 more yards in limited second-half action. Sophomore running back Ezekiel Elliott had 65 rushing yards to go with 52 receiving yards before the break, sparking OSU to a 45-0 halftime lead.

The Buckeyes' fast start was aided by two long pass plays on top of steady output from the running game. Redshirt-sophomore wide receiver Michael Thomas took a Barrett pass 63 yards for a touchdown before senior wide receiver Devin Smith scored on a 50-yard catch and run to close out the first-half for OSU.

Redshirt-senior running back Rod Smith led the first half scoring with a pair of touchdowns — the first on a short pass from Barrett and the second on the ground from a yard out.

On top of the offensive explosion, the Buckeyes' defense held the Golden Flashes to just 126 total yards as Kent State failed to crack the century mark on the ground or through the air.

Junior linebacker Joshua Perry said OSU's ability to hold Kent State to such a low number in the total yardage column made him even happier than keeping the Golden Flashes off the scoreboard.

"That's the thing that puts a smile on my face," Perry said after the game. "Shutout is one thing...but when you can hold an offense to that I think it's really impressive. Like I said, it doesn't matter who the opponent is, that's a tough thing to do." ▪

Redshirt freshman H-back Jalin Marshall catches an 18-yard pass from J.T. Barrett and launches into the end zone in the third quarter. *Mark Batke | Photo Editor*

BOX SCORE

	1	2	3	4	T
Kent State	0	0	0	0	0
Ohio State #22	21	24	14	7	66

SCORING SUMMARY

FIRST QUARTER

OSU TD 13:16 Michael Thomas 14 Yd pass from J.T. Barrett (Sean Nuernberger Kick)
Drive info: 5 plays, 58 yds in 1:44

OSU TD 9:30 Rod Smith 8 Yd pass from J.T. Barrett (Sean Nuernberger Kick)
Drive info: 9 plays, 65 yds in 2:05

OSU TD 1:49 Rod Smith 1 Yd Run (Sean Nuernberger Kick)
Drive info: 7 plays, 54 yds in 2:17

SECOND QUARTER

OSU FG 14:16 Sean Nuernberger 41 Yd Field Goal
Drive info: 5 plays, 7 yds in 1:30

OSU TD 12:43 Michael Thomas 63 Yd pass from J.T. Barrett (Sean Nuernberger Kick)
Drive info: 2 plays, 63 yds in 0:16

OSU TD 4:34 Marcus Baugh 2 Yd pass from J.T. Barrett (Sean Nuernberger Kick)
Drive info: 13 plays, 94 yds in 4:55

OSU TD 1:38 Devin Smith 50 Yd pass from J.T. Barrett (Sean Nuernberger Kick)
Drive info: 1 plays, 50 yds in 0:08

THIRD QUARTER

OSU TD 9:20 Jalin Marshall 3 Yd pass from J.T. Barrett (Sean Nuernberger Kick)
Drive info: 6 plays, 28 yds in 2:40

OSU TD 5:08 Curtis Samuel 3 Yd Run (Sean Nuernberger Kick)
Drive info: 5 plays, 32 yds in 1:55

FOURTH QUARTER

OSU TD 12:38 Curtis Samuel 1 Yd Run (Sean Nuernberger Kick)
Drive info: 12 plays, 98 yds in 5:48

NCAA NATIONAL CHAMPIONS

WIDE RECEIVERS

TEAM SUCCESS MOST IMPORTANT TO RECEIVING CORP

by Tim Moody

More than any other position group in football, wide receivers have a reputation for being divas.

At Ohio State, that reputation might not be lost when stepping into wide receivers coach Zach Smith's room.

"We definitely have divas, yes, we have divas," redshirt-freshman H-back Jalin Marshall said. "I can't tell you their names 'cause they're my brothers, but we have divas in the wide receiver room."

But for the Buckeyes — while that diva attitude might be present depending who you ask — the goals of the team come to the forefront more than individual glory, Marshall said. He added that each receiver is still ready to step into the limelight when his time comes.

"We want to win more than we want the ball," he said. "So if we do have to get the ball to win, I feel like we can make the plays that are given to us. That's why it's not so much of a battle in the room anymore, because we want to win."

Despite a plethora of different personalities at the position, Marshall credited Smith for his ability to keep the group together.

"Coach Smith, I think he handles it all well, our own little personalities," he said.

The core group of OSU's receiving corps consists of six players — two seniors in Devin Smith and Evan Spencer, a redshirt-junior in Corey Smith, redshirt-sophomore Michael Thomas, sophomore H-back Dontre Wilson and redshirt-freshman Marshall. Those players have accounted for 72 of OSU's 110 receptions this season for 1,236 yards and 15 touchdowns.

"There's probably six guys rotating right now," Zach Smith said. "All six of them, there may not be a premier, marquee guy that's going to have the national stats that put him into the top of the country category, but that's a testament to the development of those six guys in the group."

While none are well beyond the pack statistically, Thomas leads the group with 21 catches for 377 yards and is tied for the team-high with Devin Smith with five touchdown receptions.

Coach Smith said the success of the Buckeyes' receivers this season, despite none standing out from the pack, comes back down to the relationship they have with one another.

"In order for Mike Thomas to touch the ball, Jalin might not touch it as many times, but there's a great relationship between the two," he said as an example. "He wants Jalin to touch the ball. They all want to do well. At the end of the day, all they really care about is we win and we do our job."

While continued team success might still be their No. 1 priority, Spencer said he's also happy to see the success of his fellow receivers.

"When one person is doing well, everybody's doing well," he said Monday. "And we really kind of expanded on that notion. We wish the best upon everybody."

Hoping for the success of the players around them comes back to the relationship the receivers have with each other, which Marshall described as brotherhood, but the concoction of

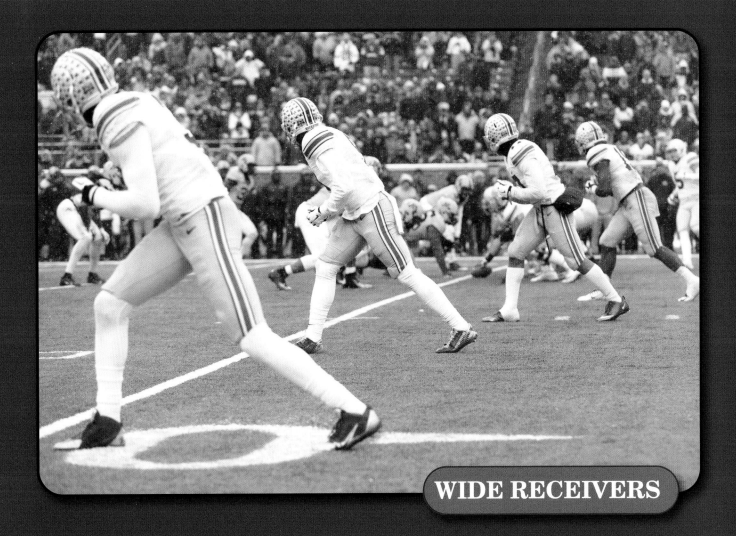

WIDE RECEIVERS

personalities might also look something like a high school homeroom.

"We got Mike Thomas, he's kind of the clown, the class clown of the room, he always makes those comments," Marshall said. "You got Evan Spencer, the leader, he's like the class president."

Marshall also called Devin Smith the "goofiest one in the room," Wilson the "class comedian," and referred to Corey Smith as a clown alongside Thomas.

"We're all fools to our own extent, we like to have fun," Spencer said.

But as for himself, Marshall painted a picture of the one who might be the model student.

"I don't know about me, I just listen to Coach Smith and go to practice, that's what I do," he said.■

JALIN MARSHALL

COREY SMITH

DEVIN SMITH

EVAN SPENCER

MICHAEL THOMAS

DONTRE WILSON

BUCKEYES
BEARCATS

50
28

Senior wide receiver Evan Spencer is all smiles after scoring a touchdown off a 19-yard pass from J.T. Barrett. *Mark Batke* | *Photo Editor*

BARRETT, BUCKEYES RUN AWAY FROM BEARCATS

Devin Smith, a senior wide receiver who all season made long catches look easy, prepares to make one of his two touchdown receptions against Cincinnati. *Mark Batke | Photo Editor*

by Tim Moody

The Ohio State football team gained more than 700 yards of total offense on its way to a 50-28 win against Cincinnati.

OSU (3-1) scored 23 points in the first quarter and another 20 in the second half to seal a 40th consecutive win against in-state opponents Saturday night at Ohio Stadium.

The Buckeyes' offensive output fueled a 30-point run in the first half and a 17-point run in the second to help negate a huge day from Cincinnati redshirt-sophomore quarterback Gunner Kiel.

With the score at 36-28 in favor of OSU in the second half, the Buckeye defense forced four consecutive punts and the offense scored two

OHIO STATE BUCKEYES

After storming onto the field surrounded by the Ohio State Marching Band—known as "The Best Damn Band in the Land"— Ohio State dominated Cincinnati, winning 50-28. *Mark Batke* | *Photo Editor*

Cincinnati's redshirt-sophomore quarterback Gunner Kiel is no match for Buckeye sophomore defensive linemen Joey Bosa, and this fumble led to an Ohio State safety in the first quarter. *Chelsea Spears | Multimedia Editor*

touchdowns in that span to take a 50-28 lead.

OSU coach Urban Meyer said he was happy with the Buckeyes' ability to move the ball, but left room for improvement from his defense. "Other than a dropped third down and a fumble, I was very pleased for the night, offensively," Meyer said after the game. "Defensively, we're back to the drawing board."

OSU redshirt-freshman quarterback J.T. Barrett powered the offensive output with 330 yards and four touchdowns. Along with Barrett's big day, the Buckeyes had a balanced attack throughout the game as they totaled 380 yards on the ground. Sophomore running back Ezekiel Elliott led all OSU ball carriers with 28 attempts for 182 yards and a touchdown.

Meyer said OSU's offense is powered by the offensive line, and said the linemen led the way to the Buckeyes' victory. "They won the game for us," Meyer said. "And they controlled that line of scrimmage, they protected our quarterback."

Kiel hit junior wide receiver Chris Moore for a 60-yard touchdown on the game's fourth play from scrimmage to put the Bearcats ahead early.

OSU responded with a run of 30 straight points — including a safety after a sack-and-strip by sophomore defensive lineman Joey Bosa.

The Cincinnati signal caller responded with two more touchdown passes toward the end of the half, including an 83-yard strike to Moore to cap a four-play, 97-yard drive. Despite the charge from Cincinnati, OSU still entered the break ahead, 30-21.

OSU junior linebacker Joshua Perry (37) stops Cincinnati junior wide receiver Alex Chisum (80). *Mark Batke | Photo Editor*

The Buckeyes opened the second half with a 14-play, 67-yard drive that ended with a 25-yard field goal by freshman kicker Sean Nuernberger to bring their lead back to double digits.

Cincinnati responded with another long touchdown from Kiel to Moore, this time for 78 yards to make it 33-28 in favor of OSU. The three connections between the pair totaled 221 yards and three touchdowns.

Meyer said he wasn't happy when the Bearcats stormed back with big plays through the air, but recognized that Cincinnati is "probably the best throwing team" OSU has faced during his tenure in Columbus.

"I asked (Cincinnati coach Tommy Tuberville) after the game, and he's got a good team," Meyer said. "But we're Ohio State, too, so we better learn how to play pass defense and get that fixed.

On the ensuing possession, OSU was forced to settle for another field goal, which Nuernberger put through the uprights from 42 yards out, extending the lead to 36-28.

After the Buckeyes' defense forced a punt, Barrett hit sophomore H-back Dontre Wilson in the end zone without a defender within five yards.

Another Cincinnati punt lead to another touchdown pass for Barrett as he hit senior wide receiver Devin Smith from 34 yards giving the Buckeyes' their final margin of victory, 50-28. ∎

OSU redshirt-sophomore quarterback Cardale Jones (12) hurdles a Maryland defender. *Mark Batke* | *Photo Editor*

BUCKEYES
TERRAPINS

52
24

OHIO STATE TOPS MARYLAND IN BIG TEN OPENER

J.T. Barrett (16) accepts congratulations from Michael Thomas (3) and Evan Spencer after one of his four touchdown passes on the day.
Mark Batke | Photo Editor

by Tim Moody

In the first-ever football matchup between Ohio State and Maryland, the No. 20 Buckeyes came away with a wire-to-wire victory to open their Big Ten season.

OSU's 52-24 win spoiled Maryland's first Big Ten home game at Byrd Stadium in College Park, Md., on Saturday afternoon.

After the win, OSU coach Urban Meyer said he was "very pleased" with the Buckeyes' play, but stressed that there is still room for improvement.

"I know it wasn't perfect; and obviously that's what you strive to be, but we're not," Meyer said.

After the Buckeyes (4-1, 1-0) jumped out to a 24-3 lead, a Maryland (4-2, 1-1) touchdown and an ensuing OSU punt near the end of the first half had the Terrapins threatening to get back in the game. That punt — a 69-yard boot by sophomore Cameron Johnston — pinned Maryland at its own seven-yard line.

Johnston said Meyer told him to put everything

OSU senior cornerback Doran Grant (12) runs after intercepting a pass. *Mark Batke* | *Photo Editor*

Michael Thomas (3) had a big day against Maryland, leading the team with four receptions for 75 yards and a touchdown.
Mark Batke | Photo Editor

he had into the punt before sending him out on the field.

"He said 'go after it,' so if he gives you permission to go after it and I'm allowed to go after it then I'm kind of happy," Johnston said after the game. "So it was good."

On the first play of the ensuing Terrapins drive, redshirt-freshman linebacker Darron Lee intercepted Maryland redshirt-senior quarterback C.J. Brown, giving OSU the ball at the one. Redshirt-freshman quarterback J.T. Barrett hit redshirt-junior tight end Nick Vannett on the next play for a touchdown, giving the Buckeyes the momentum and a 31-10 halftime lead.

Lee said the Buckeyes "needed a big play" at

that moment in the game, and added he simply watched the play unfold before making the interception.

"Eyes on the quarterback, and (sophomore defensive lineman) Joey Bosa was about to get him if he waited a half second longer," Lee said after the game.

From there, OSU outscored the Terrapins, 21-14, to seal the victory.

Lee said everyone from Meyer to the rest of his teammates was looking forward to the Maryland matchup because none of them had ever taken on the Terrapins.

"Coach was eager to play them, it was the first time he's ever played Maryland, first time we've

Urban Meyer was pleased with the effort of his Buckeyes in their first Big Ten meeting with Maryland, but acknowledged there was still room for improvement. *Mark Batke | Photo Editor*

played Maryland," he said. "We knew we had to jump out on them, they're an explosive team."

Barrett finished his day 18 of 23 on pass attempts for 267 yards and four touchdowns. He also finished second on the team with 71 rushing yards and another score. Sophomore running back Ezekiel Elliott led the way with 24 carries and 139 yards rushing while redshirt-sophomore wide receiver Michael Thomas led the team with four receptions for 75 yards and a touchdown through the air. Redshirt-junior wide receiver Corey Smith also had four receptions for 44 yards.

In total, Barrett completed passes to nine different receivers, and Meyer praised his ability, as well as the play of the players he throws to.

"J.T. Barrett is playing very well and the big thing is we can still get better," Meyer said. "The guys playing around him are pretty good too."

The Buckeye offense totaled 533 yards on the day, compared to 310 for Maryland.

Bosa keyed the OSU defense with one sack and 2.5 tackles for loss while sophomore safety Vonn Bell and junior linebacker Joshua Perry tied for the team lead with six tackles each.∎

BUCKEYES 56
SCARLET KNIGHTS 17

Ezekiel Elliott's one-yard run into the end zone resulted in the Buckeyes second of two first-quarter touchdowns. Elliott ended up rushing for 69 yards. *Mark Batke | Photo Editor*

RECORD-SETTING OFFENSE LEADS OHIO STATE PAST RUTGERS

Michael Thomas' explosive runs helped lead the Buckeyes to their fourth-straight 50-plus point game. *Mark Batke | Photo Editor*

by Tim Moody

The Ohio State football team took a 28-point lead into the half on its way to a 56-17 win against Rutgers in the first-ever matchup between the two schools.

The Buckeyes (5-1, 2-0) gained 585 yards of total offense while forcing the Scarlet Knights (5-2, 1-2) into six punts and three turnovers

Saturday at Ohio Stadium.

The Buckeyes' offensive explosion led to their fourth straight 50-plus point game, which is a school record. OSU also tied a program record with its fourth straight outing with 500 or more total yards on offense.

Even though some may expect such success to get

OHIO STATE BUCKEYES

to a team's head, coach Urban Meyer said he hasn't seen the Buckeyes get complacent so far in 2014.

"The good thing is that I don't feel like there's a complacent attitude," Meyer said after the game. "Complacency is awful in this business and with the players, because when you watch the film, we could actually have played a lot better in certain situations."

Quarterback J.T. Barrett opened the game nine for nine on pass attempts, totaling 117 yards and a pair of scores. He hit redshirt-junior tight end Nick Vannett from 12 yards out on the Buckeyes' first drive before finding Vannett again from 26 yards out to start the second quarter.

Barrett finished the first half with 147 yards through the air and another 50 on the ground, leading OSU to a 35-7 advantage through 30 minutes.

In addition to the quarterback's hot start, sophomore running back Ezekiel Elliott and redshirt-senior running back Rod Smith each had short rushing touchdowns in the first half to go along with a four-yard fumble return for a score by redshirt-freshman cornerback Eli Apple.

Rutgers was forced to punt four times in the first half while also throwing an interception and losing one fumble.

J.T. Barrett helped his own cause with a pair of rushing touchdowns, and left no doubt who was the Buckeyes offensive leader. *Mark Batke | Photo Editor*

Urban Meyer said his team was as "hungry" as the coaching staff, and that drive positioned them well for a strong run through the rest of the season. *Mark Batke | Photo Editor*

Following up on a fast start to the first half, the Buckeyes marched down the field to score a touchdown less than two minutes into the second half, extending their lead to 42-7. Barrett's 33-yard run gave OSU a 35-point lead with more than 28 minutes to play in the game.

On the Buckeyes' next drive, Barrett sparked OSU with his legs once again. On fourth-and-goal, he evaded the Scarlet Knights' pass rush to scamper in from five yards to make the lead 49-7. With more than eight minutes to play in the third quarter, the OSU signal caller had 107 rushing yards and a pair of scores to go with two touchdown tosses.

Rutgers tacked on a field goal to cap the ensuing drive, but a 42-yard pass from Barrett to senior wide receiver Devin Smith set the Buckeyes up at the Rutgers 11 on OSU's next possession.

Senior wide receiver Evan Spencer hauled in a touchdown with one hand two plays later to make it 56-10 with 19:14 to play in the game. The touchdown pass was Barrett's 20th of the season.

The Scarlet Knights answered with a touchdown drive, but their deficit was still 39 with less than a quarter to play.

Meyer said the Buckeyes will have an opportunity to "enjoy the win tonight," but added he wants his team to be focused when it comes back to practice.

"Do what you gotta do and come back ready to go," Meyer said. "The good thing (is) this is a really good team to coach right now. They're as hungry as our coaching staff and that's a good sign." ■

	1	2	3	4	T
Rutgers	7	0	3	7	17
Ohio State #13	14	21	21	0	56

SCORING SUMMARY

FIRST QUARTER

OSU   TD   11:34   Nick Vannett 12 Yd pass from J.T. Barrett (Sean Nuernberger Kick)

Drive info: 6 plays, 52 yds in 2:29

OSU   TD   5:24   Ezekiel Elliott 1 Yd Run (Sean Nuernberger Kick)

Drive info: 8 plays, 74 yds in 3:33

RUTG   TD   0:27   Desmon Peoples 1 Yd Run (Kyle Federico Kick)

Drive info: 10 plays, 66 yds in 4:57

SECOND QUARTER

OSU   TD   13:03   Nick Vannett 26 Yd pass from J.T. Barrett (Sean Nuernberger Kick)

Drive info: 6 plays, 67 yds in 2:24

OSU   TD   9:50   Eli Apple 4 Yd Fumble Return (Sean Nuernberger Kick)

Drive info: 1 plays, -1 yds in 0:08

OSU   TD   4:32   Rod Smith 3 Yd Run (Sean Nuernberger Kick)

Drive info: 8 plays, 51 yds in 3:39

THIRD QUARTER

OSU   TD   13:17   J.T. Barrett 33 Yd Run (Sean Nuernberger Kick)

Drive info: 4 plays, 79 yds in 1:43

OSU   TD   8:24   J.T. Barrett 5 Yd Run (Sean Nuernberger Kick)

Drive info: 10 plays, 55 yds in 2:58

RUTG   FG   6:36   Kyle Federico 42 Yd Field Goal

Drive info: 6 plays, 51 yds in 1:48

OSU   TD   4:14   Evan Spencer 11 Yd pass from J.T. Barrett (Sean Nuernberger Kick)

Drive info: 6 plays, 64 yds in 2:22

FOURTH QUARTER

RUTG   TD   14:54   Desmon Peoples 12 Yd Run (Kyle Federico Kick)

Drive info: 8 plays, 80 yds in 4:20

Cardale Jones's late-game action against Rutgers was just a precursor of magical things to come for the quarterback. *Mark Batke | Photo Editor*

BIG-TIME BACKFIELD

BARRETT AND ELLIOTT LEAD BUCKEYES OFFENSE

by Tim Moody

Led by redshirt-freshman quarterback J.T. Barrett and sophomore running back Ezekiel Elliott, the Ohio State football team has broken school records and dominated its opponents.

One cannot help but wonder, though, how does the Barrett-Elliott combination compare to last year's two-headed monster that was Braxton Miller and Carlos Hyde?

First, let's compare Barrett to Miller.

In his first five starts under coach Urban Meyer in 2012, Miller totaled 933 yards through the air, tallying eight passing scores to go along with three interceptions.

Barrett's stats have been even more impressive.

Despite being named the starting quarterback a month after being listed as third on the depth chart, Barrett has accumulated 1,354 yards through the air, including 17 touchdowns and five interceptions.

Meanwhile, Elliott, who has improved in games against Cincinnati and Maryland, has not put up the Hyde-like numbers Buckeye fans are used to seeing.

After sitting out the first three games of 2013 Hyde exploded during the rest of his senior campaign. In his first five games (not including the game against Florida A&M) he amassed 660 yards on the ground to go along with seven scores.

J.T. BARRETT

Elliott, who has put up back-to-back 100-plus-yard rushing games for the first time in his career, has totaled 462 yards on the ground in his first five starts as a Buckeye, while adding three scores.

Co-offensive coordinator and offensive line coach Ed Warinner said that while he is pleased with Elliott's production, he is not the same running back Hyde was when he donned the scarlet and gray.

"He's playing with very low pad level and so he plays with great energy. He's explosive," Warinner said of Elliott. "And he finishes runs with great pad level. And he doesn't want to make direct contact. He did the job you would want a Carlos Hyde to do (against Cincinnati). But he's a different runner than Carlos."

While the Miller-Hyde combo led the Buckeyes to an undefeated regular season in 2013, the Barrett-Elliott connection is helping produce a more balanced offense.

Following the 2013 campaign, the Buckeyes ranked fifth nationally in rushing offense while finishing 90th in pass offense.

The 2014 season has produced much different results so far as the Buckeyes currently rank 19th in rush offense and sit 36th in the country in pass offense.

Meyer said the Buckeyes strive for balance on offense.

"What I think is going on best is the balance right now. When you start looking up at the scoreboard and you see 250 or 300 (yards) each that's a good sign," Meyer said Wednesday. "The last two years have been kind of run-dominated, and to win those big games, you can't be 220 run and 68 pass. You're going to lose that game."

While the Buckeyes have in fact lost a game with Barrett and Elliott occupying the backfield, the improvements being made since the embarrassing loss to Virginia Tech seem to be giving Buckeye players, coaches and fans hope for the future.■

EZEKIEL ELLIOTT

BUCKEYES   31
NITTANY LIONS   24

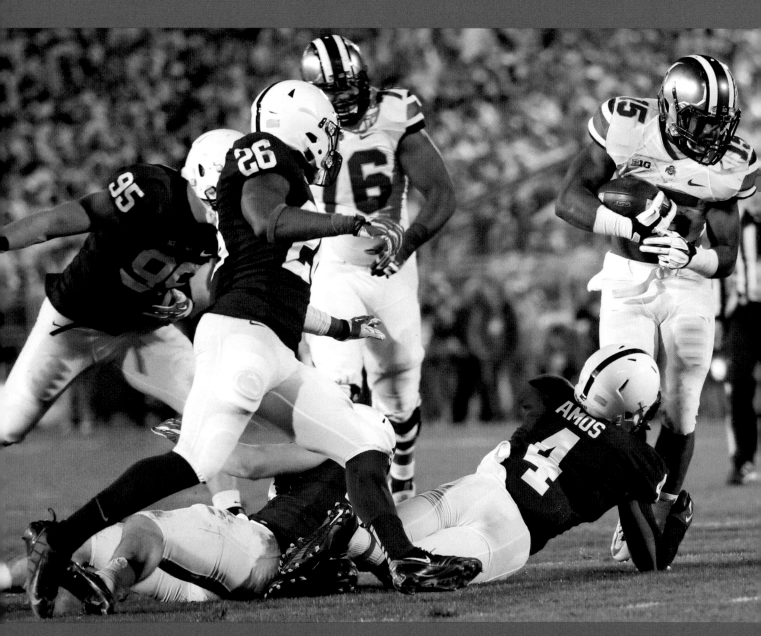

Ezekiel Elliott got the Buckeyes on the board early against Penn State with a touchdown in the first quarter, and helped the running game continue to flourish. *Mark Batke | Photo Editor*

JOEY BOSA CEMENTS DOUBLE-OVERTIME WIN FOR BUCKEYES

The OSU football team storms the field as Penn State players head for the locker room following a 31-24 double-overtime win by the Buckeyes.
Mark Batke | Photo Editor

by Tim Moody

The No. 13 Ohio State football team jumped out to an early lead, but relied on a late defensive stand in a 31-24 double-overtime victory against Penn State.

OSU (6-1, 3-0) sophomore defensive lineman Joey Bosa knocked down Penn State (4-3, 1-3) sophomore quarterback Christian Hackenberg on fourth-and-five in the second overtime to seal the win Saturday

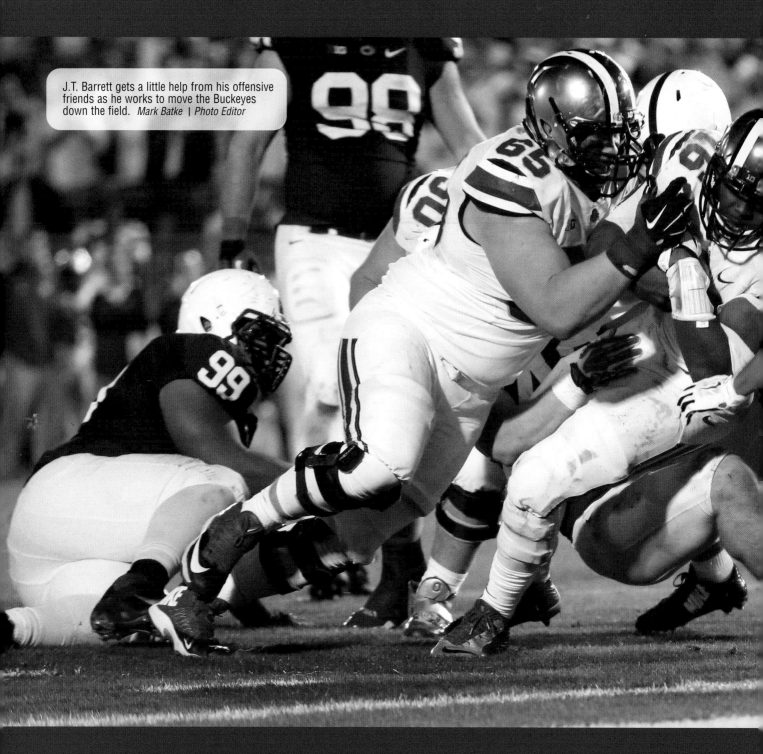

J.T. Barrett gets a little help from his offensive friends as he works to move the Buckeyes down the field. *Mark Batke | Photo Editor*

night at Beaver Stadium.

"I think we learned that we are a real team, and when adversity strikes we can come together and win a big game in a crazy environment," Bosa said after the game.

After the Buckeyes outscored the Nittany Lions 17-0 in the first half, Penn State reversed field in the second half to tie the game at 17 with nine seconds on the clock to force overtime.

OSU coach Urban Meyer saved praise for his team's opponent after the game, and added that the Buckeyes need to improve their play along the line.

"A credit to our opponent, they played their tails off," Meyer said. "Outplayed us up front, I think. (I'm) a little upset with the way we played up front and we got to get that fixed."

Penn State got the ball first in overtime as Hackenberg led the Nittany Lions to a first-and-goal from the two-yard line. The Buckeyes held on to force third down at the one, but senior running back Bill Belton found his way into the end zone to give Penn State its first lead of the night.

On the Buckeyes' first overtime possession, redshirt-freshman quarterback J.T. Barrett kept

the Buckeyes forced fourth-down–and-five at the 20. Hackenberg was knocked to the ground as Bosa overpowered a Nittany Lion blocker.

Bosa — who said he "needed to play a lot better" — finished the game with 2.5 sacks and six total tackles.

Barrett said he was simply glad Bosa was wearing a white jersey rather than Penn State's blue shirt in the game.

"Joey Bosa, one thing I can say, I'm really glad he's on our team," he said. "That's for sure. Great player."

The double-overtime finish came after Penn State picked up a late field goal on a drive that began inside its own 10-yard line.

Barrett threw his second interception on OSU's first play of the fourth quarter, and the Penn State offense managed to break through on the next drive.

After the pick, Hackenberg hit freshman wide receiver Saeed Blacknall for a 24-yard touchdown, moving the Nittany Lions within three points.

Penn State forced OSU to punt on the next drive, but senior wide receiver Devin Smith downed it at the one-yard line. The Nittany Lions were forced to punt, giving the ball back to the OSU offense with 51 yards between it and the end zone, and 5:17 remaining on the clock.

The OSU drive stalled forcing a punt and Hackenberg led the Nittany Lions to the OSU 43-yard line before being sacked by Bosa on first down. A penalty against the Buckeyes on the next play gave Penn State a new set of downs on the OSU 28, needing just a field goal to force overtime.

On third-and-six at the OSU 14 yard-line with 19 seconds on the clock Hackenberg threw incomplete into the end zone, forcing a 31-yard field goal attempt that Nittany Lions senior kicker Sam Ficken drilled to force overtime.

Sophomore running back Ezekiel Elliott paced the Buckeyes' offense with 26 carries for 109 yards and a touchdown, while Barrett added 20 carries for 75 yards and his two overtime scores. The OSU signal caller also finished the game 12-for-19 for 74 yards with one touchdown and two interceptions. Senior tight end Jeff Heuerman led the Buckeyes with three receptions for 19 yards and a score.

Elliott said jumping out to a 17-0 lead was a positive, but giving the lead away was disappointing.

"We took the crowd away in the first half. In the second half, we just didn't have any momentum at all and the crowd got back into it and we started to make some mistakes," Elliott said after the game. "It was crazy. I wouldn't say it was quite the atmosphere of (Ohio Stadium) but it was crazy."■

the ball on a second-and-seven to set up first and goal from the five with a 17-yard run. He kept it again on the next play, scoring a touchdown to tie the game at 24.

Due to a personal foul penalty against Penn State following the Buckeyes' extra point, OSU started the second overtime at the 12-yard line. Barrett led the Buckeyes to a third-and-two at the four-yard line, before taking another quarterback keeper into the end zone to put OSU back on top, 31-24.

Penn State took over at the 25-yard line, but

Darron Lee (43) celebrates after a sack of Penn State sophomore quarterback Christian Hackenberg. *Mark Batke | Photo Editor*

OHIO STATE BUCKEYES

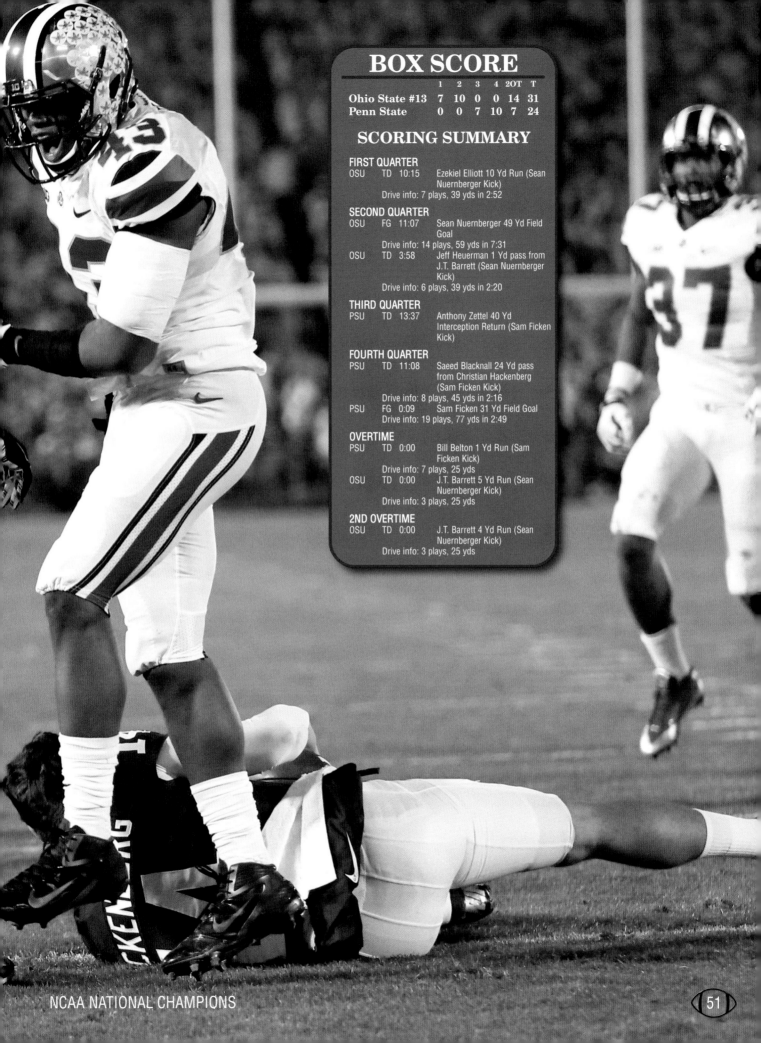

BOX SCORE

	1	2	3	4	2OT	T
Ohio State #13	7	10	0	0	14	31
Penn State	0	0	7	10	7	24

SCORING SUMMARY

FIRST QUARTER
OSU   TD   10:15   Ezekiel Elliott 10 Yd Run (Sean Nuernberger Kick)
Drive info: 7 plays, 39 yds in 2:52

SECOND QUARTER
OSU   FG   11:07   Sean Nuernberger 49 Yd Field Goal
Drive info: 14 plays, 59 yds in 7:31
OSU   TD   3:58   Jeff Heuerman 1 Yd pass from J.T. Barrett (Sean Nuernberger Kick)
Drive info: 6 plays, 39 yds in 2:20

THIRD QUARTER
PSU   TD   13:37   Anthony Zettel 40 Yd Interception Return (Sam Ficken Kick)

FOURTH QUARTER
PSU   TD   11:08   Saeed Blacknall 24 Yd pass from Christian Hackenberg (Sam Ficken Kick)
Drive info: 8 plays, 45 yds in 2:16
PSU   FG   0:09   Sam Ficken 31 Yd Field Goal
Drive info: 19 plays, 77 yds in 2:49

OVERTIME
PSU   TD   0:00   Bill Belton 1 Yd Run (Sam Ficken Kick)
Drive info: 7 plays, 25 yds
OSU   TD   0:00   J.T. Barrett 5 Yd Run (Sean Nuernberger Kick)
Drive info: 3 plays, 25 yds

2ND OVERTIME
OSU   TD   0:00   J.T. Barrett 4 Yd Run (Sean Nuernberger Kick)
Drive info: 3 plays, 25 yds

BUCKEYES
FIGHTING ILLINI

55
14

Redshirt-senior offensive lineman Darryl Baldwin (left) congratulates and Curtis Samuel on one of his two touchdowns.
Mark Batke | *Photo Editor*

BARRETT, JONES LEAD OHIO STATE PAST ILLINOIS

J.T. Barrett (16) attempts to escape pressure from the Illinois defense. *Mark Batke | Photo Editor*

by Tim Moody

With a matchup against a top-10 opponent on the horizon, the No. 13 Ohio State football team used Illinois as a nice tune up in their 55-14 win Saturday night.

Despite OSU's scheduled game against No. 8 Michigan State being just a week away, coach Urban Meyer said his team didn't have any issues focusing on the task at hand, and praised the performance of his defense in particular.

"I think we have a good bunch of players that care about each other and get ready for a big week," Meyer said after the game. "So I thought our defense came out and played really well."

But despite the strong performance on defense, Meyer added the OSU offense had room to improve after posting 55 points but finishing four-of-six in the red zone and zero-for-two on fourth down attempts.

"A little disappointed in the red zone offense, couple of field goals we could have probably

The Illini defense was no match for Devin Smith, as he catches a 32-yard pass from J.T. Barrett.
Mark Batke | Photo Editor

kicked or we could have gone for," he said. "But I still want to put a lot of pressure on our offensive line and quarterback in those kinds of situations because we know more moments like that are coming down the road."

Room for improvement aside, the Buckeyes'

win at Ohio Stadium marked their 20th straight regular-season Big Ten victory, tying the conference record set by OSU between 2005 and 2007.

After totaling 31 points through regulation and two overtimes against Penn State last week, the Buckeyes (7-1, 4-0) jumped out to a 31-0 advantage

in the first half against the Fighting Illini (4-5, 1-4).

With redshirt-freshman quarterback J.T. Barrett nursing a sprained MCL, Meyer elected to go with redshirt-sophomore quarterback Cardale Jones to start the second half.

Jones hit sophomore H-back Dontre Wilson for a 27-yard touchdown on his opening drive, pushing the lead to 38-0. The play marked the first touchdown toss of Jones' OSU career.

After an OSU field goal, sophomore defensive lineman Joey Bosa sacked Illinois senior quarterback Reilly O'Toole on third down to force

Michael Thomas helps the Ohio State offense score 55 points, with this fourth-quarter touchdown catch from Cardale Jones. *Mark Batke* | *Photo Editor*

OHIO STATE BUCKEYES

a punt. On the third play of the ensuing drive, redshirt-freshman H-back Jalin Marshall scored a 30-yard touchdown after taking the shotgun snap, pushing the lead to 48-0.

With the Buckeyes' backups on the field on defense, the Fighting Illini broke the shutout on their next drive with a five-yard touchdown run from senior running back Donovonn Young.

Jones came right back and hit redshirt-sophomore wide receiver Michael Thomas for another touchdown to open the fourth quarter, making it 55-7. The Fighting Illini added one more touchdown in the fourth quarter, but OSU ran out the clock to seal the win.

The Buckeyes forced three first-half turnovers from Illinois, including a pair of interceptions thrown by O'Toole.

"It feels great to get the turnovers and the energy it brings our team," redshirt-freshman linebacker Darron Lee, who had one of the interceptions, said after the game. "We've been working so hard and it's a lot of fun."

Barrett and Jones combined to throw for 249 yards and four touchdowns as the Buckeyes outgained Illinois, 545 to 243 overall. Smith led the team with 72 receiving yards and a pair of scores, while Elliott rushed for a game-high 69 yards.

Junior linebacker Joshua Perry tallied a team-high seven total tackles and Bosa recorded two sacks. ∎

OSU players sing 'Carmen Ohio' following a game against Illinois. *Mark Batke | Photo Editor*

BOX SCORE

	1	2	3	4	T
Illinois	0	0	7	7	14
Ohio State #16	17	14	17	7	55

SCORING SUMMARY

FIRST QUARTER

OSU TD 11:25 Curtis Samuel 23 Yd Run (Sean Nuernberger Kick)
Drive info: 3 plays, 38 yds in 0:38

OSU FG 6:47 Sean Nuernberger 44 Yd Field Goal
Drive info: 9 plays, 48 yds in 2:54

OSU TD 1:30 Devin Smith 32 Yd pass from J.T. Barrett (Sean Nuernberger Kick)
Drive info: 9 plays, 71 yds in 3:47

SECOND QUARTER

OSU TD 11:43 Curtis Samuel 1 Yd Run (Sean Nuernberger Kick)
Drive info: 6 plays, 24 yds in 2:41

OSU TD 0:20 Devin Smith 8 Yd pass from J.T. Barrett (Sean Nuernberger Kick)
Drive info: 2 plays, 25 yds in 0:14

THIRD QUARTER

OSU TD 11:56 Dontre Wilson 27 Yd pass from Cardale Jones (Sean Nuernberger Kick)
Drive info: 8 plays, 79 yds in 3:04

OSU FG 9:31 Sean Nuernberger 26 Yd Field Goal
Drive info: 4 plays, 5 yds in 1:37

OSU TD 7:20 Jalin Marshall 30 Yd Run (Sean Nuernberger Kick)
Drive info: 3 plays, 51 yds in 0:54

ILL TD 1:48 Donovonn Young 5 Yd Run (David Reisner Kick)
Drive info: 11 plays, 65 yds in 5:32

FOURTH QUARTER

OSU TD 14:21 Michael Thomas 19 Yd pass from Cardale Jones (Sean Nuernberger Kick)
Drive info: 7 plays, 50 yds in 2:27

ILL TD 5:55 Matt LaCosse 7 Yd pass from Aaron Bailey (David Reisner Kick)
Drive info: 8 plays, 44 yds in 2:47

JOEY BOSA

A DOMINATING PRESENCE

by Tim Moody

When Ohio State's Joey Bosa drilled Cincinnati quarterback Gunner Kiel earlier in the year and forced a fumble that ultimately resulted in a safety, the record crowd at Ohio Stadium erupted.

Bosa wasn't even sure where the ball landed.

"I just made a move inside and my eyes got big and I ran as fast as I can and hit him as hard as I could," Bosa, a sophomore defensive lineman, said following the game. "I actually thought he got the ball off so I stood up and went to walk back to the line, but I saw the ball pop out."

The play not only electrified the fans and gave OSU a 16-7 lead, but it seemed to ignite the defense for a stretch in the first quarter as the Buckeyes forced the Bearcats into two straight punts.

Co-defensive coordinator and linebackers coach Luke Fickell said that the play of Bosa, who leads the Buckeyes with 2.5 sacks, is at least partially because of his 6-foot-5-inch, 278-pound frame.

"He is a very dominating force. He is a guy who has the speed to get the edge, but he's got the power to do some things inside," Fickell said. "It is an unbelievable combination. I haven't seen a whole lot of guys like it, but we are still going to expect him to continue to grow."

Coach Urban Meyer acknowledged Bosa's physical skills, but added the Fort Lauderdale, Fla., product is also successful because of his upbringing.

"He just goes, he practices that way from day one. It's a product of his family. His dad's got an incredible football background," Meyer said. "I thought we'd have a guy that would be pretty much game-ready because he went to a really quality high school program."

Bosa's high school, St. Thomas Aquinas, has been known to produce high-quality football talent, including former OSU safety Nate Salley, former Wisconsin player and current New England Patriot running back James White and former Chicago Bear Brian Piccolo, who was the inspiration for the movie "Brian's Song."

Meyer also said that while he believed Bosa would be ready to play coming out of high school, he is still impressed with how the sophomore has performed so far.

"I didn't imagine him to be this ready," Meyer said. "He's extremely strong and quick and relentless. And on top of that, he loves and understands the game."

Meyer has coached an impressive array of defensive linemen in his coaching career, including two at Florida who were first-round draft picks — Jarvis Moss, Denver in 2007 and Derrick Harvey, Jacksonville in 2008. However, he said Bosa reminds him most of a player he has coached at OSU.

"I think he's similar to John Simon. He's a little more talented than John, a little longer," Meyer said. "But John Simon had that same relentlessness — you watch those two play in practice and compete and there's a mindset.

"Those are two good people to be in company, everybody knows how we all feel about John Simon. But to even mention someone in that same vein, who is a few inches taller and a little longer, that's pretty rare air, those two guys."

Meyer's comparison could be spot on, as Simon led the Buckeyes in sacks during his senior season in Columbus, something Bosa is on pace to do just two years later.

With such high praise and potential, Fickell said he, along with the rest of the coaching staff, is expecting even more from Bosa.

"The sky is the limit for that guy with his abilities. We are going to continue to put things upon his shoulders," Fickell said. "He goes hard, he is physical, he does all the things we ask him to do, now we are going to ask him to continue to grow — strive for greatness and not be satisfied with where he is." ∎

JOEY BOSA

BUCKEYES 49
SPARTANS 37

OHIO STATE FINDS REDEMPTION IN VICTORY OVER MICHIGAN STATE

by Tim Moody

EAST LANSING, Mich. — Eleven months and a day after Michigan State beat Ohio State in the 2013 Big Ten Championship game, the No. 13 Buckeyes overcame an early deficit to top the No. 7 Spartans, 49-37.

The win put the Buckeyes (8-1, 5-0) alone atop the Big Ten East Division standings, breaking a tie with Michigan State (7-2, 4-1). OSU also set a conference record with its 21st consecutive regular season Big Ten win.

"It was a great opportunity for two good football teams to go play, and I'm very proud of our guys," OSU coach Urban Meyer said after the game. "A young team grew up tonight."

Sophomore running back Ezekiel Elliott said OSU came into the game with a chip on its shoulder, and added the Buckeyes wanted to prove their doubters wrong.

"Just coming into this game, no one believed in us," he said. "We had no one behind our back besides Buckeye nation and ourselves. We just had to come out and prove to the world that we're ready."

Heading into the weekend, the Buckeyes were ranked No. 14 in the College Football Playoff rankings, while the Spartans were No. 8.

Senior defensive lineman Michael Bennett said beating Michigan State means OSU's "dreams are still alive for this year." He added the game was about playing for the future, rather than getting revenge for last year's loss.

"It's about accomplishing what we can accomplish this year," Bennett said after the

Facing Page: (From right) Urban Meyer; his wife, Shelly; offensive lineman Pat Elflein; and tight end Jeff Heuerman sing 'Carmen Ohio', and rejoice in a hard-fought victory over Michigan State, redeeming a 2013 loss in the Big Ten Championship.
Mark Batke / Photo editor

Above: Dontre Wilson catches a 7-yard touchdown pass in the fourth quarter.
Mark Batke / Photo editor

J.T. Barrett's quick feet prove just as dangerous as his cannon-like arm, as he keeps the Buckeyes moving against Michigan State's defense.
Mark Batke / Photo editor

Darron Lee, a dominating defensive force all season, celebrates a stop of the Spartans.
Mark Batke / Photo editor

game. "And so by having that big win over a really good team, it really just keeps everything alive and starts putting us in the conversation."

In a first half filled with momentum swings, OSU found a way to take a 28-21 advantage into the locker rooms — thanks in part to four total touchdowns from quarterback J.T. Barrett.

After both teams scored early in the first quarter, OSU muffed a punt and Michigan State Jeremy Langford scored from 33 yards out on the first play of the ensuing drive.

Barrett answered with his second touchdown run of the night on fourth-and-goal at the one, but Langford scored again to make it 21-14, set up by a key third-and-23 pass to senior wide receiver Devin Smith for a gain of 43 yards.

OSU sophomore H-back Dontre Wilson fumbled on the ensuing kick to give the ball back to the Spartans, but they missed a 39-yard field goal to give OSU the ball on its own 21-yard line.

On the opening play of the next drive, Barrett hit redshirt-sophomore wide receiver Michael Thomas for a 79-yard touchdown to tie the game at 21.

After a Michigan State punt, Barrett went deep again and found Smith for a 44-yard touchdown, capping a five-play, 64-yard go-ahead drive for the Buckeyes.

The 28-21 halftime lead came despite a pair of fumbles and six penalties for OSU.

Michigan State opened the final 30 minutes with a field goal, but a 13-play OSU drive was capped by a one-yard touchdown run from Elliott, making it 35-24 with 2:18 to play in the third quarter.

The Buckeyes stopped Michigan State on fourth-and-five on the ensuing drive, taking over at their own 36 to start the fourth.

OSU marched down the field in less than three minutes before Barrett hit Wilson for a seven-yard touchdown to make it 42-24 with 12:07 to play. Michigan State redshirt-junior quarterback Connor Cook responded with a 16-yard touchdown strike to sophomore tight end Josiah Price.

After Elliott's touchdown, the Spartans took it back down the field for a touchdown, but Cook's two-point conversion attempt fell short, keeping a 12-point advantage for OSU with 5:20 to play.

Barrett finished the game with exactly 300 passing yards and three touchdowns and added another 86 yards and two scores on the ground. Elliott led all players with 154 rushing yards while Smith totaled 129 yards receiving.

"We just tried to forget about the mistakes, because mistakes happen in games," Barrett said after the game. "Those were...big mistakes, wish

we didn't make 'em, but we did. We just all had to respond as a team and just get back together and play football."

Meyer, who is not known to sensationalize a win, said the win over the Spartans was "one for the ages."

"That's how much respect we had for our opponent going into it. We played a top-10 team and we really played our best and on the road," Meyer said. "Once again, I look at our players and I see how many young guys are playing for us that are going to be around here for awhile. So, the future's pretty bright." ▪

BOX SCORE

	1	2	3	4	T
Ohio State #14	7	21	7	14	49
Michigan St #8	14	7	3	13	37

SCORING SUMMARY

FIRST QUARTER
MSU TD 9:42 — Keith Mumphery 15 Yd pass from Connor Cook (Michael Geiger Kick)
Drive info: 5 plays, 70 yds in 2:02
OSU TD 8:41 — J.T. Barrett 5 Yd Run (Sean Nuernberger Kick)
Drive info: 4 plays, 71 yds in 1:01
MSU TD 6:14 — Jeremy Langford 33 Yd Run (Michael Geiger Kick)
Drive info: 1 plays, 33 yds in 0:06

SECOND QUARTER
OSU TD 12:27 — J.T. Barrett 1 Yd Run (Sean Nuernberger Kick)
Drive info: 8 plays, 50 yds in 3:21
MSU TD 4:37 — Jeremy Langford 1 Yd Run (Michael Geiger Kick)
Drive info: 14 plays, 66 yds in 7:50
OSU TD 3:19 — Michael Thomas 79 Yd pass from J.T. Barrett (Sean Nuernberger Kick)
Drive info: 1 plays, 79 yds in 0:11
OSU TD 0:56 — Devin Smith 44 Yd pass from J.T. Barrett (Sean Nuernberger Kick)
Drive info: 5 plays, 64 yds in 1:03

THIRD QUARTER
MSU FG 8:38 — Michael Geiger 40 Yd Field Goal
Drive info: 12 plays, 56 yds in 6:22
OSU TD 2:18 — Ezekiel Elliott 1 Yd Run (Sean Nuernberger Kick)
Drive info: 13 plays, 67 yds in 6:20

FOURTH QUARTER
OSU TD 12:07 — Dontre Wilson 7 Yd pass from J.T. Barrett (Sean Nuernberger Kick)
Drive info: 6 plays, 64 yds in 2:53
MSU TD 9:15 — Josiah Price 16 Yd pass from Connor Cook (Michael Geiger Kick)
Drive info: 7 plays, 75 yds in 2:52
OSU TD 7:12 — Ezekiel Elliott 17 Yd Run (Sean Nuernberger Kick)
Drive info: 4 plays, 78 yds in 2:03
MSU TD 5:20 — Jeremy Langford 1 Yd Run (Two-Point Pass Conversion Failed)
Drive info: 10 plays, 76 yds in 1:52

Taylor Decker (66) and Pat Elflein share a hug after their work on the offensive line helped the Buckeyes defeat Michigan State.
Mark Batke / Photo editor

BUCKEYES
GOPHERS

31
24

Amid the cold and snow, Urban Meyer works to fire up his Buckeye team.
Mark Batke / Photo editor

RECORD-SETTING J.T. BARRETT HELPS OHIO STATE HOLD MINNESOTA

J.T. Barrett carries the ball past Minnesota defenders on his way to a 189-yard day on the ground, scoring a touchdown and setting three school records. Mark Batke / Photo editor

by Tim Moody

MINNEAPOLIS — Ohio State quarterback J.T. Barrett broke multiple school records as the Buckeyes held on for a 31-24 win against Minnesota Saturday afternoon at TCF Bank Stadium.

The redshirt-freshman broke the OSU single-season record for total touchdowns when he found redshirt-sophomore wide receiver Michael Thomas in the third quarter for his 37th touchdown on the year. He also set school records for the longest run by a quarterback with an 86-yard touchdown in the first quarter and the

Ezekiel Elliott celebrates with Buckeye Nation after his team defeats Minnesota.
Mark Batke / Photo editor

Evan Spencer catches a 22-yard pass from J.T. Barrett and charges into the end zone to stretch the Buckeyes' fourth-quarter lead to 31-14 over Minnesota.
Mark Batke / Photo editor

most rushing yards by a quarterback with 189.

Co-offensive coordinator and quarterbacks coach Tom Herman said after the game that Barrett is a player the Buckeyes can "lean on when the game gets tight."

Coach Urban Meyer said the performance continued to show what kind of player the Wichita Falls, Texas, native can be after he entered the season relatively unknown.

"Early in the season, we had no idea who J.T. Barrett was. We have a very clear picture now," Meyer said after the game.

Despite Barrett's big day, three turnovers — two fumbles and one interception — by OSU (9-1, 6-0) kept Minnesota (7-3, 4-2) in the game down to the wire.

The Buckeyes built a 14-0 lead in the first quarter after Barrett scored on his 86-yard touchdown run and found H-back Jalin Marshall for a 57-yard score. But a Barrett interception and Marshall's first lost fumble led to two touchdowns from Gopher running back David Cobb.

Despite taking just a three-point lead into the break, OSU outgained the Golden Gophers, 354-133, in the opening 30 minutes.

Herman said the Buckeyes can't turn the ball over to achieve their ultimate goals, but praised the team for finding a way to hang on.

"You can't take those turnovers away. They are what they are, and that's what made the game close," he said. "But I was proud of our guys to continue to battle back and continue to make plays."

Despite struggling at times, Meyer called OSU's performance a "great team win."

"Not great execution, but great team win," he said. "It was a tough environment against a very good team that we have a lot of respect for."

After the Golden Gophers responded to an early deficit, OSU bounced back with 10 unanswered points to take a 24-14 advantage into the final 15 minutes.

OSU sophomore safety Vonn Bell intercepted Minnesota quarterback Mitch Leidner early in the fourth quarter, giving the Buckeyes the ball in Golden Gopher territory.

On the ensuing drive, Barrett found senior wide receiver Evan Spencer from 22 yards out for a touchdown, making it 31-14 with 10:08 to play.

OSU forced a punt on the ensuing drive, but Marshall fumbled after signaling for a fair

catch, giving the Golden Gophers the ball in the red zone. Two plays later, Cobb scored his third touchdown of the day to bring Minnesota within 10.

All three Minnesota touchdowns came on drives following OSU turnovers.

OSU punted on the ensuing drive, and the Golden Gophers drove down to the Buckeyes' 17-yard line. Minnesota converted on a 34-yard field goal on second-and-10, but OSU recovered the onside kick and ran down the clock to seal the seven-point victory.

In addition to his 189 yards on the ground, Barrett had 200 passing yards and four total touchdowns. Sophomore running back Ezekiel Elliott totaled 91 rushing yards while Marshall led the Buckeyes with 95 receiving yards.

Barrett's three passing touchdowns give him 29 on the season, just one away from tying the OSU record set by Troy Smith during his Heisman Trophy winning season in 2006. ∎

BOX SCORE

	1	2	3	4	T
Ohio State #8	14	3	7	7	31
Minnesota #25	0	14	0	10	24

SCORING SUMMARY

FIRST QUARTER
OSU   TD 10:14   J.T. Barrett 86 Yd Run (Sean Nuernberger Kick)
Drive info: 3 plays, 95 yds in 1:17
OSU   TD 4:33   Jalin Marshall 57 Yd pass from J.T. Barrett (Sean Nuernberger Kick)
Drive info: 8 plays, 87 yds in 3:32

SECOND QUARTER
MINN   TD 14:27   David Cobb 5 Yd Run (Ryan Santoso Kick)
Drive info: 5 plays, 39 yds in 1:59
MINN   TD 1:24   David Cobb 30 Yd Run (Ryan Santoso Kick)
Drive info: 11 plays, 80 yds in 6:08
OSU   FG 0:00   Sean Nuernberger 22 Yd Field Goal
Drive info: 10 plays, 57 yds in 1:24

THIRD QUARTER
OSU   TD 7:37   Michael Thomas 30 Yd pass from J.T. Barrett (Sean Nuernberger Kick)
Drive info: 6 plays, 65 yds in 2:55

FOURTH QUARTER
OSU   TD 10:08   Evan Spencer 22 Yd pass from J.T. Barrett (Sean Nuernberger Kick)
Drive info: 6 plays, 32 yds in 2:34
MINN   TD 7:08   David Cobb 12 Yd Run (Ryan Santoso Kick)
Drive info: 2 plays, 14 yds in 0:48
MINN   FG 1:19   Ryan Santoso 34 Yd Field Goal
Drive info: 9 plays, 63 yds in 1:15

BUCKEYES 42
HOOSIERS 27

Jalin Marshall was just getting started when he returned this punt for a touchdown in the third quarter. He went on to score three more consecutive touchdowns.
Mark Batke / Photo editor

JALIN MARSHALL SPARKS SECOND-HALF COMEBACK

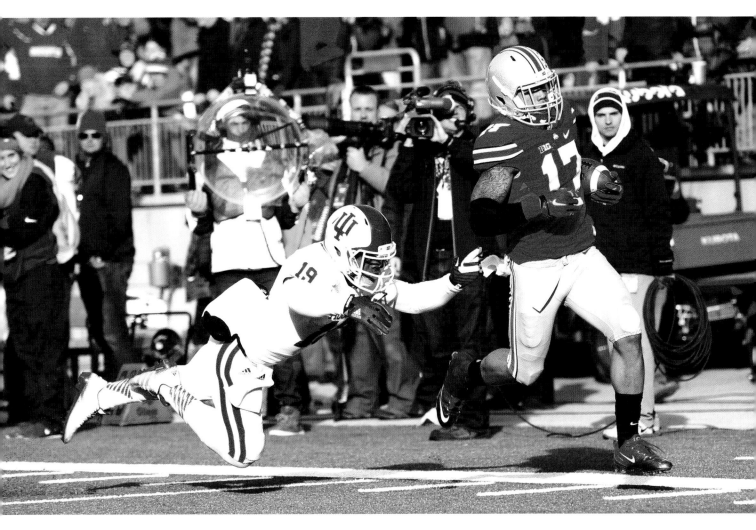

Jalin Marshal evades Indiana freshman safety Tony Fields for a another touchdown. Mark Batke / Photo editor

by James Grega, Jr.

For the large part of Ohio State's game against Indiana, the Buckeyes, along with most of the crowd of 101,426 at Ohio Stadium, seemed to be sleeping through the icy conditions in Columbus.

It took until 2:20 left in the third quarter for both parties to wake up.

With OSU down 20-14, and not having scored since its second drive of the first quarter, redshirt-freshman H-back Jalin Marshall took an Indiana punt 54 yards for a score to give OSU the lead and the Buckeyes did not look back as they defeated the Hoosiers 42-27.

Marshall said he thought he had to make something happen in order to spark the OSU

J.T. Barrett's control of the game at all levels helped make him a Heisman Trophy candidate.
Mark Batke / Photo editor

Sophomore safety Vonn Bell makes sure the Indiana offense does not get anything going, as the Buckeyes roll over the Hoosiers, 42-27.
Mark Batke / Photo editor

comeback.

"They (Indiana) were pinned real deep, and I felt like I had to make a play to turn this game around for the team," Marshall said. "It felt real good after I did that."

Even though Marshall committed two turnovers in a 31-24 win over Minnesota last week, OSU coach Urban Meyer said he never worried about Marshall's ability.

"He's a talented guy. I think that was good for his confidence," Meyer said. "He's going to be around here a while; only a freshman and very talented freshman. Carrying a lot of the load."

With the win, the Buckeyes clinched their second straight appearance in the Big Ten Championship Game, something Meyer said was gratifying, but he acknowledged there is room for improvement.

"We're conference division champions, won a bunch of games in a row," he said. "We still have some work to do."

The Buckeyes started fast as sophomore running back Ezekiel Elliott took off untouched for a 65-yard touchdown less than two minutes into the game, and it looked as though the Buckeyes were well on their way to an easy win.

But after trading punts to start the third quarter, the Hoosiers took the lead on a 90-yard touchdown run by talented junior running back Tevin Coleman to make the score 20-14 with 7:17 remaining in the quarter.

Meyer said that the crowd, along with his team became complacent after scoring the first 14 points of the game.

"Sometimes in college football, things don't go exactly as scripted, and (we) kind of went out, jumped out to 14-0 lead and the stadium was dead and we were dead," Meyer said.

But after Marshall's punt return gave the Buckeyes the lead back, the Middletown, Ohio, native prepared for an encore performance.

Marshall added three more scores after the return, as he caught quarterback J.T. Barrett's school record-breaking pass for passing scores in a season from six yards out to extend the OSU lead to 28-20. Then, Marshall hauled in a one-handed catch from Barrett for a 15-yard touchdown with 4:21 left in the game giving the Buckeyes a two-score lead.

He also took a touch-pass from Barrett 54-yards for a touchdown less than two minutes later to conclude the Buckeye scoring.

BOX SCORE

	1	2	3	4	T
Ohio State #6	14	0	7	21	42
Indiana	10	3	7	7	27

SCORING SUMMARY

FIRST QUARTER
OSU TD 13:49 Ezekiel Elliott 65 Yd Run
(Sean Nuernberger Kick)
Drive info: 3 plays, 76 yds in 1:11
OSU TD 8:28 Jeff Heuerman 4 Yd pass from
J.T. Barrett (Sean Nuernberger Kick)
Drive info: 9 plays, 65 yds in 4:34
IND TD 6:41 Tevin Coleman 2 Yd Run
(Griffin Oakes Kick)
Drive info: 5 plays, 65 yds in 1:47
IND FG 4:41 Griffin Oakes 30 Yd Field Goal
Drive info: 6 plays, 18 yds in 1:51

SECOND QUARTER
IND FG 9:34 Griffin Oakes 37 Yd Field Goal
Drive info: 7 plays, 59 yds in 2:54

THIRD QUARTER
IND TD 7:17 Tevin Coleman 90 Yd Run
(Griffin Oakes Kick)
Drive info: 1 plays, 90 yds in 0:13
OSU TD 2:20 Jalin Marshall 54 Yd Punt Return
(Sean Nuernberger Kick)
Drive info: 3 plays, 3 yds in 1:05

FOURTH QUARTER
OSU TD 13:03 Jalin Marshall 6 Yd pass from
J.T. Barrett (Sean Nuernberger Kick)
Drive info: 11 plays, 76 yds in 3:33
OSU TD 4:21 Jalin Marshall 15 Yd pass from
J.T. Barrett (Sean Nuernberger Kick)
Drive info: 1 plays, 15 yds in 0:04
OSU TD 2:49 Jalin Marshall 54 Yd pass from
J.T. Barrett (Sean Nuernberger Kick)
Drive info: 1 plays, 54 yds in 0:09
IND TD 1:13 Tevin Coleman 52 Yd Run
(Griffin Oakes Kick)
Drive info: 3 plays, 71 yds in 1:36

Marshall said it was relieving to play so well after struggling against the Golden Gophers a week earlier.

"It's definitely a little bit of redemption. It does feel good to have it off my back and move away from all the negatives of last week," he said.

After being included by many in the Heisman Trophy discussion, Barrett threw for 302 yards and four touchdowns. Barrett also threw two interceptions for the first time since a win over Penn State on Oct. 25.

Elliott, who surpassed 1,000 yards on the season on his first carry of the game, finished with 107 rushing yards and a score to go along with 39 yards receiving. ∎

KOSTA KARAGEORGE

KOSTA KARAGEORGE 'MADE EVERY DAY ENJOYABLE' FOR BUCKEYE TEAMMATES

by Tim Moody

Even as a high school wrestler at Pickerington North, Pat Eflein knew he wanted nothing to do with Kosta Karageorge on the mat.

"I remember he was wrestling the district finals match," Ohio State's redshirt-sophomore offensive lineman said. "And I was like, 'Wow, I don't wanna wrestle that guy.'"

Elflein said he was a high school freshman at the time, but six years later, he's the Buckeyes' starting right guard. Karageorge, on the other hand, walked on to the football team in August after wrestling for three seasons at OSU.

Last Wednesday, Karageorge was reported missing by his family, and on Sunday his body was discovered near his Columbus apartment. Police said the cause of death appeared to be a self-inflicted gunshot wound, and a coroner said Karageorge might have died on Friday.

The players learned of their teammate's death after practice on Sunday, and Elflein said it was hard to believe.

"He was a great person, you know, it's really shocking to hear that news," he said. "Our prayers are with his family and with him. The kid just, every day, came out with the same positive attitude, no matter what the circumstances were."

During his weekly press conference, Coach Urban Meyer said the loss of life was an "incredible tragedy." Meyer added that Karageorge "loved" his time as a football player at OSU.

While Elflein said he had only known Karageorge personally since he joined the team, some other OSU players had known him longer. Junior offensive lineman Taylor Decker said he

A police poster showing Kosta Karageorge, an Ohio State player who has been missing since earlier in the week, is displayed on the large video board at the south end of the field before the start of the Ohio State vs. Michigan game. *Jay LaPrete | AP Photo*

Members of the Ohio State football team arrive at The Annunciation Greek Orthodox Cathedral for the funeral of Ohio State football player Kosta Karageorge Wednesday, Dec. 3, 2014, in Columbus, Ohio. *Jay LaPrete | AP Photo*

met Karageorge two years ago through mutual friends, and stressed the important role he played for the team.

After hearing the news of his teammate's death, Decker said he spent Sunday night hoping it wasn't true.

"I know I was thinking about it all night, and you just kind of wake up and hope it was all a nightmare," Decker said. "Just for somebody that you've been with every day for months and months, just, it's sad, it's sad."

Decker added that Karageorge was a "blue-collar American guy," and said he was always positive. Decker said the two hit it off because they had a lot in common — like their interest in tattoos — and said Karageorge had talked about wanting to be a WWE wrestler.

Karageorge's position mate — senior Michael Bennett — said his late teammate always came to practice with a smile on his face, saying "how thankful he is to be a part of the football team

and to be able to go practice with us."

Bennett added that Karageorge was a spark plug before practice started.

"He would always just — right before practice — start yelling 'yeah baby,' and just be pumped up and it would make everybody else excited for practice," Bennett said. "He made every day enjoyable."

Elflein added that Karageorge's death puts football in perspective, and adds more focus to what is happening off the field.

"It just makes me think of Kosta and what he would want," Elflein said. "I already told you what kind of guy he was, and thinking about that I know he wouldn't want us to go downhill from this. Kosta wants us to win that game, and beat them and win a ring. And get Kosta a ring, he deserves it because he's put in the work.

"I just kind of think of 'what would Kosta want?' He wants a championship, so we're gonna get it." ∎

BUCKEYES 42
WOLVERINES 28

The Michigan defense had no chance against Ezekiel Elliott, who scored his second touchdown of the game off this 44-yard run.
Mark Batke / Photo editor

BARRETT INJURED AS OHIO STATE TOPS MICHIGAN

by Tim Moody

With holding just a seven-point lead in the fourth quarter against , a record crowd at Ohio Stadium fell nearly silent.

Redshirt-freshman quarterback J.T. Barrett — thought by many to be a leading Heisman Trophy candidate — was down on the field with trainers huddled around him. Barrett wound up being carted off the field after sustaining what appeared to be a right leg injury.

After the game, OSU released a statement saying Barrett's injury is a fractured right ankle that will keep him on the sidelines for the rest of the season.

Redshirt-sophomore quarterback Cardale Jones replaced Barrett and the defense came up big in the second half as OSU (11-1, 8-0) topped the Wolverines (5-7, 3-5) for the third consecutive season and eliminated from bowl-game contention in front of 108,610 fans at the Horseshoe.

Coach Urban Meyer said he was honored as he became the first Buckeye coach to beat in each of their first three seasons in since the 1930s.

"We'll take that as a coaching staff and team," Meyer said after the game. "That's a hell of an honor."

After tying the game just before halftime, OSU took a 21-14 lead on the opening drive of the second half with Barrett's second rushing touchdown in as many drives.

 responded with a touchdown of its own, set up by an 18-yard pass from redshirt-sophomore running back Drake Johnson to redshirt-senior quarterback Devin Gardner. But in a game of swings,

Curtis Grant, celebrating after a tackle, was just one member of a dominating Buckeye defense that seemed to get stronger as the season went on.
Mark Batke / Photo editor

J.T. Barrett was leading his first Buckeye victory over Michigan when a broken ankle ended his season.
Mark Batke / Photo editor

It may have been the last game in Ohio Stadium for an emotional Evan Spencer, but the Buckeye season was far from over.
Mark Batke / Photo editor

the Buckeyes took the lead back minutes later with a two-yard touchdown run by Ezekiel Elliott.

After Barrett's injury and a Jones failed third-down run, the Buckeye defense took a bend-but-don't-break stance, forcing a Wolverine punt that bounced into the end zone for a touchback. Elliott's touchdown run on the next drive extended OSU's lead to 14 with 4:58 remaining.

The Buckeyes scored again exactly a minute later when redshirt-freshman linebacker Darron Lee picked up a fumble and ran 33 yards for a touchdown. The fumble was forced by defensive lineman Joey Bosa as he sacked .

The late second-half surge for OSU came after an opening 30 minutes in which the Buckeyes were outgained, 203 yards to 176.

was intercepted by sophomore safety Vonn Bell on the second play of the game, setting the Buckeyes up in Wolverine territory.

OSU's ensuing drive was capped off by a touchdown pass from Barrett to redshirt-junior tight end Nick Vannett to put the team ahead 7-0. After two sacks by OSU forced a punt on its next drive, the Buckeyes stalled and momentum swung in the Wolverines' favor.

found sophomore tight end Jake Butt on a 12-yard touchdown to tie the game before a drive that lasted more than seven minutes put the visitors ahead with 7:34 to play in the first half.

OSU punted on its next possession, but a holding penalty and a sack by senior defensive lineman Michael Bennett forced into a third-and-29 and an eventual punt. The Buckeyes took over with 2:15 to play before the break.

Barrett capped OSU's drive with a 25-yard touchdown scamper to tie the game at 14 going into the half.

Meyer said he considered running out the clock going into halftime, but changed his mind and it paid off for the Buckeyes.

"(Former college football coach) Lou Holtz always said the last five minutes of the first half, first five minutes of the second half, that's where all the momentum is," Meyer said. "And we went into the locker room with a lot of

momentum."

Before leaving the game, Barrett had 176 passing yards and another 89 on the ground. Elliott ran for 121 yards and two touchdowns on 17 carries while senior wide receiver Devin Smith led OSU with 52 receiving yards on one catch.

Barrett's touchdown pass to Vannett was his 43rd total touchdown of the season, giving him sole possession of the Big Ten record. Through 12 games as the starter, Barrett has accounted for 45 touchdowns.

Jones finished the game two for three on pass attempts for seven yards and had two carries for another 18 yards. ▪

BOX SCORE

	1	2	3	4	T
Ohio State #6	7	7	14	14	42
Michigan	7	7	7	7	28

SCORING SUMMARY

FIRST QUARTER
OSU TD 11:34 Nick Vannett 6 Yd pass from J.T. Barrett (Sean Nuernberger Kick)
Drive info: 6 plays, 41 yds in 2:38
MICH TD 2:42 Jake Butt 12 Yd pass from Devin Gardner (Matt Wile Kick)
Drive info: 7 plays, 80 yds in 3:26

SECOND QUARTER
MICH TD 7:34 Drake Johnson 2 Yd Run (Matt Wile Kick)
Drive info: 15 plays, 95 yds in 7:13
OSU TD 0:07 J.T. Barrett 25 Yd Run (Sean Nuernberger Kick)
Drive info: 10 plays, 83 yds in 2:08

THIRD QUARTER
OSU TD 12:58 J.T. Barrett 2 Yd Run (Sean Nuernberger Kick)
Drive info: 5 plays, 72 yds in 2:02
MICH TD 7:41 Drake Johnson 4 Yd Run (Matt Wile Kick)
Drive info: 12 plays, 75 yds in 5:17
OSU TD 1:08 Ezekiel Elliott 2 Yd Run (Sean Nuernberger Kick)
Drive info: 14 plays, 81 yds in 6:33

FOURTH QUARTER
OSU TD 4:58 Ezekiel Elliott 44 Yd Run (Sean Nuernberger Kick)
Drive info: 8 plays, 80 yds in 3:27
OSU TD 3:58 Darron Lee 33 Yd Fumble Return (Sean Nuernberger Kick)
Drive info: 3 plays, 11 yds in 1:00
MICH TD 1:15 Freddy Canteen 3 Yd pass from Devin Gardner (Matt Wile Kick)
Drive info: 9 plays, 75 yds in 2:43

BUCKEYES
BADGERS

59
0

Coach Urban Meyer shares the Stagg Championship Trophy with, from left, Evan Spencer, Darryl Baldwin and Doran Grant (hands on trophy) after the Buckeye's 59-0 win over Wisconsin in the Big Ten Championship game Dec. 6 in Indianapolis.
Chelsea Spears / Multimedia editor

BUCKEYES BLANK WISCONSIN 59-0 TO WIN BIG TEN CHAMPIONSHIP

by Tim Moody

INDIANAPOLIS — With a quarterback making his first collegiate start under center, the Ohio State football team shut out Wisconsin, 59-0, to lock up its first-ever Big Ten Championship Game victory.

Cardale Jones was under center after redshirt-freshman quarterback J.T. Barrett was ruled out for the season after fracturing his ankle against Michigan last week. A day after Barrett's injury, the Buckeyes also learned of the death of teammate Kosta Karageorge, who had been reported missing the previous Wednesday.

Senior defensive lineman Michael Bennett said the Buckeyes stayed together through the tumultuous week on their way to their blowout victory.

"People say that's our third-string quarterback — well, he did pretty well," Bennett said after the game. "The team rallied around him, they rallied around Kosta, and just came out and performed."

OSU (12-1, 8-0) topped the Badgers (10-3, 7-1) on Saturday night in Indianapolis after the Buckeyes fell to Michigan State, 34-24, in the conference title game in 2013.

The Buckeyes — ranked No. 5 in the College Football Playoff standings — locked up their 35th Big Ten title with the win over the No. 13 Badgers.

"It's an honor to represent the Big Ten as the champion of this great conference," OSU coach Urban Meyer said after the game. "Very proud of our team."

The game marked the first shutout in the four-year history of the Big Ten Championship Game and the first time the Badgers had been shutout since a 34-0 loss to Syracuse in 1997.

Jones finished the game 12 of 17 on pass attempts for 257 yards and three touchdowns and was named the game's MVP. But even with his accolade, Jones said he enjoyed picking up the win as a group.

"It was very fun, going out there showing

Senior defensive lineman Michael Bennett wore No. 53 while celebrating his sack of Wisconsin quarterback Joel Stave during the Big Ten Championship Game, but he soon switched to No. 63 in honor of teammate Kosta Karageorge, who was found dead just days before the game.
Mark Batke / Photo editor

Darron Lee is in hot pursuit of Wisconsin redshirt-junior running back Melvin Gordon.
Mark Batke / Photo editor

Sophomore safety Vonn Bell (11) intercepts a pass from Wisconsin redshirt-junior quarterback Joel Stave during the Big Ten Championship Game.
Mark Batke / Photo editor

everybody what we can do when we all come together as one," he said.

OSU needed less than two minutes to take a 7-0 lead. On just his third attempt of the game, Jones found Devin Smith for a 39-yard touchdown to cap a six-play, 77-yard drive.

After Wisconsin punted, the Badgers' defense got a stop, but OSU sophomore punter Cameron Johnston's kick traveled 73 yards to the Wisconsin two-yard line. The Badgers couldn't move past their own 36 on the drive, kicking it back to OSU.

On the second play of the ensuing drive Ezekiel Elliott scampered for an 81-yard touchdown run, putting the Buckeyes up, 14-0.

A 23-yard field goal by Nuernberger made it 17-0 after the first 15 minutes before OSU tacked on three more touchdowns in the second quarter to take a 38-0 lead into halftime.

The Buckeyes outgained the Badgers 364-91 in the half as Jones completed 10 of his first 13 passes for 211 yards and two touchdowns. Elliott totaled 150 yards on 12 carries and tallied two touchdowns of his own in the opening 30 minutes.

The Buckeyes remained red hot to start the third quarter as Jones found Smith again for a 42-yard touchdown. The play — which was the third scoring connection between the Buckeyes' duo — extended OSU's lead to 45-0 and cemented the win. Smith totaled four receptions for Big Ten title-game record 137 yards and three touchdowns.

The Buckeyes held Wisconsin running back and Heisman Trophy candidate Melvin Gordon to just 76 rushing yards on 26 carries. He also had a fumble that was returned for a touchdown by OSU sophomore defensive lineman Joey Bosa.

While Gordon was being shut down by the OSU defense, Elliott broke the Big Ten title game rushing record of 216 yards (previously held by Gordon) by tallying 220 yards on 20 carries.

Elliott said the attention Gordon had coming into the game helped him play with a chip on his shoulder.

"Just trying to come out there and make a name for myself," Elliott said after the game. "I knew it was a big stage, I knew everyone was going to be watching Melvin so I just wanted to come out and compete with him."

An interception by senior cornerback Doran Grant late in the third quarter set the Buckeyes up in Wisconsin territory, but the drive stalled and a field goal try from freshman kicker Sean Nuernberger was blocked.

After a Wisconsin punt, the Buckeyes made it 52-0 after a 60-yard run by Elliott set up a 12-yard touchdown scamper by freshman running back

Curtis Samuel.

Grant recorded another interception in the fourth quarter, and Samuel scored again on the ensuing drive for the final points of the game.

Bennett — normally No. 63 — wore No. 53 against the Badgers in honor of Karageorge. He had two sacks and forced the fumble that led to Bosa's touchdown.

The Buckeyes also wore No. 53 stickers on their helmets and there was a moment of silence in Karageorge's honor before the game.

Karageorge — an OSU wrestler turned football walk-on — was found dead last Sunday.

Meyer said the Buckeyes also had their own moment to honor Karageorge before taking the field.

"There's a family grieving that was a big part of our family," Meyer said. "Kosta, we had a prayer and a moment of silence in our locker room for him and his family. We'll never forget our teammate." ∎

BOX SCORE

	1	2	3	4	T
Ohio State #5	0	0	0	0	0
Wisconsin # 13	14	24	7	14	59

SCORING SUMMARY

FIRST QUARTER

OSU TD 13:01 Devin Smith 39 Yd pass from Cardale Jones (Sean Nuernberger Kick)

Drive info: 6 plays, 77 yds in 1:59

OSU TD 4:06 Ezekiel Elliott 81 Yd Run (Sean Nuernberger Kick)

Drive info: 2 plays, 93 yds in 0:42

SECOND QUARTER

OSU FG 14:14 Sean Nuernberger 23 Yd Field Goal

Drive info: 7 plays, 53 yds in 2:41

OSU TD 11:09 Devin Smith 44 Yd pass from Cardale Jones (Sean Nuernberger Kick)

Drive info: 3 plays, 63 yds in 1:17

OSU TD 6:36 Ezekiel Elliott 14 Yd Run (Sean Nuernberger Kick)

Drive info: 6 plays, 69 yds in 2:52

OSU TD 0:36 Joey Bosa 4 Yd Fumble Return (Sean Nuernberger Kick)

Drive info: 4 plays, -1 yds in 1:40

THIRD QUARTER

OSU TD 9:24 Devin Smith 42 Yd pass from Cardale Jones (Sean Nuernberger Kick)

Drive info: 5 plays, 77 yds in 2:47

FOURTH QUARTER

OSU TD 11:39 Curtis Samuel 12 Yd Run (Sean Nuernberger Kick)

Drive info: 2 plays, 72 yds in 0:34

OSU TD 2:25 Curtis Samuel 1 Yd Run (Sean Nuernberger Kick)

Drive info: 7 plays, 61 yds in 4:02

Cardale Jones (12) and Joey Bosa celebrate with the Stagg Championship Trophy following the Buckeyes win. Credit: Chelsea Spears / Multimedia edito

BUCKEYES 42
CRIMSON TIDE 35

As Urban Meyer accepts the Sugar Bowl trophy (fourth from left), Michael Thomas soaks in the celebratory environment.

OHIO STATE STORMS BACK TO ROLL ALABAMA

by Tim Moody

NEW ORLEANS — Ohio State booked its ticket to the first-ever College Football Playoff National Championship after coming back from a 15-point deficit to top No. 1 Alabama in the Sugar Bowl.

Redshirt-freshman linebacker Darron Lee said the Buckeyes proved they belong among the nation's elite with the 42-35 victory.

"We're back. We're back," Lee said after his defensive MVP performance. "Those that thought we were gone, we're back. Be afraid, be very afraid."

Coach Urban Meyer agreed with Lee and added that his team validated its ability.

"They're good enough," Meyer said after the game. "That was a sledgehammer game. That was a classic, so we are good enough."

After falling behind, 21-6, in the first half, the No. 4 Buckeyes scored 28 unanswered points before holding off a late surge from No. 1 Alabama to win Thursday night in New Orleans.

OSU (13-1, 8-0) extended its national-best winning streak to 12 games as it beat the Crimson Tide (12-2, 7-1) to improve its official record to 2-2 all time in the Sugar Bowl.

Just over two minutes into the second half, OSU redshirt-sophomore quarterback Cardale Jones found senior wide receiver Devin Smith for a 47-yard touchdown, giving the Buckeyes a 27-21 advantage and their first lead since going up 3-0 early.

Alabama coach Nick Saban said his team took the big lead based off important plays at key moments, but added it wasn't dominating the game.

"We were up 21-6 because of two turnovers and two stops in the red zone," Saban said after the game. "So, we really weren't stopping them. We kind of had the momentum of the game because of the turnovers that we got and converted those into scores."

Cardale Jones made it two-for-two as Ohio State's starting quarterback, after leading the Buckeyes to a Sugar Bowl victory and a shot at the national title.
Mark Batke / Photo editor

Whether on the ground or in the air, Cardale Jones shows Alabama he is a force to be reckoned with.
Mark Batke / Photo editor

The Buckeyes worked to take advantage of every Alabama mistake, like this interception grabbed by Tyvis Powell (23). Mark Batke / Photo editor

Despite out-gaining the Crimson Tide, 348-139, in total yards in the first half, the Buckeyes found themselves trailing, 21-20, at the break.

An early 54-yard run by sophomore running back Ezekiel Elliott put the Buckeyes in the red zone on their first drive, but the Alabama defense held, forcing an OSU field goal.

After the game, Meyer said he feels Elliott deserves more praise than he gets in the national picture.

"He's probably the most underrated back in the country," Meyer said.

The Buckeyes' next four drives ended with a fumble, another field goal, a punt and an interception, paving the way for the Crimson Tide to take a 21-6 lead with 8:07 to play in the half. But OSU responded with a 12-play, 71-yard drive, capped by a three-yard touchdown run by Elliott, making it 21-13.

Alabama was forced into its fourth three-and-

Senior defensive lineman Steve Miller (88) returns an interception for a touchdown, helping to ensure a Buckeye victory.
Mark Batke / Photo editor

NCAA NATIONAL CHAMPIONS

Michael Thomas (3) makes a touchdown
reception as Alabama junior cornerback
Cyrus Jones (5) looks on.
Mark Batke / Photo editor

Devin Smith's long catches have become legendary among Buckeye Nation.
Mark Batke / Photo editor

out on the ensuing drive, but pinned OSU at its own 23-yard line with 1:32 to play.

The Buckeyes moved the ball to the Alabama 13-yard line, and OSU called a reverse pass, leading to a 13-yard scoring toss from senior wide receiver Evan Spencer to redshirt-sophomore wide receiver Michael Thomas, which brought the Buckeyes to within one point after 30 minutes of play.

After Smith's 47-yard score early in the third quarter the teams traded punts on the next two possessions before Alabama committed its first turnover of the night. OSU senior defensive lineman Steve Miller intercepted redshirt-senior quarterback Blake Sims and returned it 41 yards for a touchdown. The pick-six gave the Buckeyes a 34-21 lead with 3:21 to play in the third quarter.

Sims responded with a five-yard touchdown run of his own, pulling Alabama back within six points.

The Crimson Tide caught a break with 9:53 to play in the game when OSU sophomore punter Cameron Johnston's kick traveled just 21 yards, giving Alabama the ball at the Buckeye 23-yard line. But Sims was intercepted by sophomore safety Vonn Bell — a former Alabama recruit — on the first play of the drive, giving OSU the ball with 9:44 to play.

Alabama pinned the Buckeyes at their own five-yard line with a punt with 5:24 on the clock, but Elliott found a hole on the fourth play of the drive and scampered 85 yards for a touchdown. The ensuing 2-point conversion from Jones to Thomas put OSU ahead, 42-28, with just 3:24 remaining in the game.

Sims found junior wide receiver Amari Cooper for a six-yard touchdown on the ensuing drive, but Spencer recovered the onside kick, allowing the Buckeyes to take possession.

Alabama forced another OSU punt, but with eight seconds to play, Sims' last-ditch attempt from 42 yards out was intercepted by redshirt-sophomore safety Tyvis Powell, sealing the Buckeye victory.

Sims praised the OSU defense after the game and chose to shoulder the blame for his team's loss.

"Ohio State's a great defense. They played with a lot of passion today," Sims said. "The way they played we didn't have good looks here and there. And the things that didn't happen good for the team I take full responsibility for it, because it's probably something that I could have did better to help my team win."

Elliott finished the game with 230 yards — a Sugar Bowl record — on 20 carries with two touchdowns while Jones threw for 243 yards and another score. Thomas led the Buckeyes with seven receptions, and Smith led all players with 87 receiving yards.

BOX SCORE

	1	2	3	4	T
Ohio State #4	6	14	14	8	42
Alabama #1	14	7	7	7	35

SCORING SUMMARY

FIRST QUARTER
OSU FG 11:32 Sean Nuernberger 22 Yd Field Goal
Drive info: 10 plays, 80 yds in 2:26
ALA TD 9:25 Derrick Henry 25 Yd Run (Adam Griffith Kick)
Drive info: 2 plays, 33 yds in 0:28
OSU FG 5:17 Sean Nuernberger 21 Yd Field Goal
Drive info: 11 plays, 71 yds in 4:08
ALA TD 2:06 Amari Cooper 15 Yd pass from Blake Sims (Adam Griffith Kick)
Drive info: 8 plays, 79 yds in 3:11

SECOND QUARTER
ALA TD 8:07 T.J. Yeldon 2 Yd Run (Adam Griffith Kick)
Drive info: 5 plays, 15 yds in 2:02
OSU TD 2:55 Ezekiel Elliott 3 Yd Run (Sean Nuernberger Kick)
Drive info: 12 plays, 71 yds in 5:12
OSU TD 0:12 Michael Thomas 13 Yd pass from Evan Spencer (Sean Nuernberger Kick)
Drive info: 6 plays, 77 yds in 1:20

THIRD QUARTER
OSU TD 12:44 Devin Smith 47 Yd pass from Cardale Jones (Sean Nuernberger Kick)
Drive info: 6 plays, 75 yds in 2:16
OSU TD 3:21 Steve Miller 41 Yd Interception Return (Sean Nuernberger Kick)
Drive info: Unavailable
ALA TD 1:01 Blake Sims 5 Yd Run (Adam Griffith Kick)
Drive info: 7 plays, 84 yds in 2:20

FOURTH QUARTER
OSU TD 3:24 Ezekiel Elliott 85 Yd Run (Cardale Jones Pass to Michael Thomas for Two-Point Conversion)
Drive info: 4 plays, 95 yds in 2:00
ALA TD 1:59 Amari Cooper 6 Yd pass from Blake Sims (Adam Griffith Kick)
Drive info: 6 plays, 65 yds in 1:25

Elliott — who was named the offensive MVP — said he came in ready to play after hearing praise for Alabama's running game.

"(Former Oklahoma State and Detroit Lions running back) Barry Sanders said before the game there were two great running backs that were going to play tonight, and they both were for Bama," Elliott said. "I felt a little bit left out."

OSU is set to take on No. 2 Oregon in the College Football Playoff National Championship on Jan. 12 at AT&T Stadium in Arlington, Texas.

Elliott said the Buckeyes have to turn their focus to the championship right away to finish the season strong.

"Gotta go back out there, grind, finish this how we want to," he said. ∎

Ezekiel Elliott breaks toward the end zone and one of his two touchdowns on the day.
Mark Batke / Photo editor

URBAN MEYER

MEYER & BUCKEYES SET SIGHTS ON HIGH-FLYING OREGON IN NATIONAL CHAMPIONSHIP MATCHUP

by Tim Moody

While he cracked a half smile as he said it, Urban Meyer's words after finding out the score of Oregon's semifinal matchup with Florida State held significant meaning.

"I gotta go," the Ohio State coach said when told that the No. 2 Ducks shellacked the No. 3 Seminoles, 59-20. "We gotta go get ready for that one."

Jokes aside, the No. 4 Buckeyes are set for just 11 days of preparation for a College Football Playoff National Championship clash with Oregon after beating No. 1 Alabama, 42-35, Thursday in the Sugar Bowl.

OSU finds itself with a shot at a national title to cap off a tumultuous season that saw Heisman candidate and senior quarterback Braxton Miller go down with a season-ending injury just 12 days before the first game. By week two, the Buckeyes had already suffered their first loss of the season, and by the end of the Michigan game had lost a second Heisman candidate in quarterback J.T. Barrett, who broke his ankle in the win.

After the win over Alabama, defensive lineman Michael Bennett said the Buckeyes showed up in New Orleans with the title game already on their mind, and added he and his teammates won't struggle to stay focused.

"We played this game to play the next game, so I think everybody's minds are already on the next game," Bennett said. "I don't think it's gonna be hard to refocus people. Guys didn't see this game as the end, we saw this game as the next step."

For OSU to even have a shot at that next step, it had to overcome a series of adverse circumstances. Outside of the week two loss to Virginia Tech — and the injuries to Miller and Barrett — the Buckeyes played the Big Ten Championship Game less than a week after learning of the death of teammate Kosta Karageorge.

On the back of redshirt-sophomore quarterback Cardale Jones, OSU beat Wisconsin, 59-0, to pick up the conference title before toppling to top-ranked Crimson Tide at the Mercedes-Benz Superdome.

"It is definitely unreal from the situation I was in to the situation my team was in," Jones said after the Sugar Bowl victory. "I mean, beginning of the season into the middle of the season and then now."

Jones added that the Ducks' convincing margin of victory against Florida State won't change the Buckeyes' game plan when it comes to preparing for the title bout, but he added the team will still take note.

"It's just impressive," Jones said. "To go out there and beat a great team like Florida State."

With the result of the Rose Bowl in mind, Bennett was quick with responses like "speed" and "fast paced" when asked what stands out about the Ducks, but he added that the Buckeyes can

COACH URBAN MEYER

match Oregon's athleticism.

"I think we have the same speed as them, but their tempo is hard to prepare for, so that's going to be the biggest thing," Bennett said. "But once you prepare for it and you're ready for it, I mean it's just another team."

But even if OSU can think of Oregon as "just another team," the Buckeyes are set to be underdogs for the third consecutive game when the two teams match up for national bragging rights, and Bennett said his team is ready for that.

"I'm sure somehow we're not gonna be good enough and we're gonna be underdogs," he said. "But that's how it goes, so we're just gonna go out there and play the game, and see what happens."▪

The Ohio State band performs prior to the College Football National Championship game against Oregon Monday, Jan. 12, 2015, in Arlington, Texas. *Tony Gutierrez | AP Photo*

OHIO STATE BUCKEYES

NATIONAL

Pregame photos by *Mark Batke* | *Photo Editor*

CHAMPIONS

Ohio State's Jalin Marshall catches a pass with Oregon's Erick Dargan (4) defending during first half action.
Brandon Wade | AP Photo

BUCKEYES 42
DUCKS 20

OHIO STATE BUCKEYES

BUCKEYES RUN PAST DUCKS TO WIN SCHOOL'S 8TH NATIONAL CHAMPIONSHIP

Wide receiver Devin Smith (9) makes a tough catch on a pass defended by Oregon defensive back Reggie Daniels (8).
Cal Sports Media | *AP Photo*

by Tim Moody

O hio State's 13th win in a row was the one that mattered most as the Buckeyes toppled No. 2 Oregon to win the first-ever College Football Playoff National Championship under the lights in North Texas.

After falling behind in the opening minutes, No. 4 OSU piled up 21 straight first-half points before sophomore running back Ezekiel Elliott led a second-half surge that culminated with a 42-20 victory. Elliott finished the game with a

Ezekiel Elliott (15) breaks the tackle of Oregon defensive back Chris Seisay (12) on his way to one of his four touchdowns on the night.
Icon Sportswire | AP Photo

Inset: Elliott celebrates his touchdown run with his teammates. Elliott finished the day with 36 carries for 246 yards and four touchdowns.
Brandon Wade | AP Photo

OHIO STATE BUCKEYES

Ohio State tight end Nick Vannett (81) makes a 1-yard touchdown reception during the first quarter to put the Buckeyes up 14-7. *Eric Gay | AP Photo*

national championship game record 246 yards and four touchdowns Monday night at AT&T Stadium.

Elliott said after the game that the Buckeyes had reached their goal, and he could barely believe it.

"This is a surreal moment," he said. "It's why we all came here. After all we went through, this is crazy. It doesn't feel real."

Redshirt-sophomore quarterback Cardale Jones said the win was even sweeter because the Buckeyes fought through injuries to two Heisman trophy-candidate quarterbacks, an early-season loss to Virginia Tech and the death of teammate Kosta Karageorge to get there.

"Long story short, we weren't supposed to be here," he said. "We had every — all the odds were stacked against us through the whole season, and for us to be sitting right here as national champs, it only means a lot to me, but our community, Buckeye nation, and our hometowns."

The Buckeyes (14-1, 8-0) picked up the eighth national title in program history, and improved to

9-0 all-time against the No. 2 Ducks (13-2, 8-1).

Elliott was named the game's offensive player of the game, while redshirt-sophomore safety Tyvis Powell picked up the defensive equivalent.

The win gave OSU its first national title since 2002 and moved coach Urban Meyer to 3-0 all-time in national title games. Meyer is just the second coach to win national championships at more than one school, as he won two while coaching at Florida.

"The chase is complete," Meyer said after the game. "These guys accepted their final mission and did it. It was our final mantra the past few weeks and I'm very grateful for the work these guys put in."

Meyer — an Ashtabula, Ohio, native and former Cincinnati football player — said he's honored to win his third championship, this time for his home state.

"I played college football here, and to bring now a national title to the great state of Ohio, it's

OHIO STATE BUCKEYES

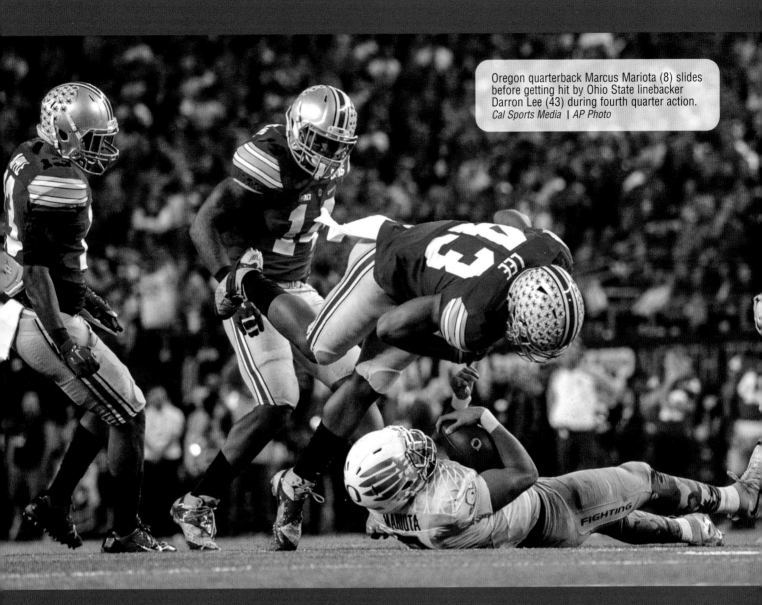

Oregon quarterback Marcus Mariota (8) slides before getting hit by Ohio State linebacker Darron Lee (43) during fourth quarter action.
Cal Sports Media | AP Photo

almost surreal," he said.

Jones — who started all three of OSU's postseason games after redshirt-freshman J.T. Barrett fractured his ankle — dedicated the win to the Buckeye seniors, who had not won a bowl game before this season.

"It's even better than I thought. It's an unreal feeling," Jones said after the game. "The seniors never could win a bowl game in four years. This is for them."

The game started with redshirt-junior quarterback and Heisman Trophy winner Marcus Mariota leading his team down the field to take an 7-0 lead after just 2:39. Jones took over at his own 25-yard line.

The teams traded punts on the next two drives, before Elliott weaved through the Oregon defense for a 33-yard touchdown, tying the game at seven with 4:36 to play in the first quarter.

OSU scored again on its next drive after an Oregon punt, taking a 14-7 lead on a touchdown

pass from Jones to redshirt-junior tight end Nick Vannett.

After an Oregon punt and a Jones fumble, the Ducks drove down to the OSU three-yard line, but came up short on fourth down. OSU fumbled on the next drive, but a sack of Mariota by junior defensive lineman Adolphus Washington forced a three-and-out for Oregon.

OSU took a 21-10 halftime lead, but Oregon pulled within one in the second half. Elliott tacked on a touchdown late in the third quarter and another in the fourth to extend the margin, helping the Buckeyes stay ahead, despite turning the ball over four times.

Meyer said the win came in part because of the play of Elliott and the offense, but stressed the importance of the improved play of the OSU defense as well.

"And it's also a testimony to the improvement our defense has made," he said. "We won that game because of course Zeke Elliott and of course

Ohio State's Cardale Jones powers his way in for a 1-yard touchdown during second quarter action. Jones touchdown along with the PAT gave the Buckeyes a 21-7 lead. *Tony Gutierrez | AP Photo*

OHIO STATE BUCKEYES

Ezekiel Elliott carries Oregon linebacker Derrick Malone Jr. (22) into the end zone to score a fourth quarter touchdown that put the Buckeyes ahead 42-20. *Cal Sports Media | AP Photo*

Cardale Jones looks for running room as Ducks linebacker Rodney Hardrick (48) closes in for the tackle. *Brandon Wade | AP Photo*

our offensive line, but our defense, to hold (Mariota) — I know he threw for a bunch of yards, 300-plus yards, but our defense, we tackled tonight and did a great job."

A fumble on OSU's second drive of the second half marked the team's fourth turnover of the game and second in the third quarter.

A defensive stand inside the 10-yard line by the Buckeyes forced an Oregon field goal with 6:39 to play in the third quarter, making it 21-20.

After the field goal, Elliott ran for 44 of 75 yards on a 12-play drive, capped by a nine-yard

scoring run to give the Buckeyes a 28-20 lead at the start of the fourth quarter. Elliott piled on another 20 yards on OSU's next drive, and punched in his third touchdown of the game to make it 35-20 with 9:44 on the clock.

Oregon coach Mark Helfrich said Elliott is a "tremendous player," and credited the OSU offensive line for some of his success against the Ducks.

"He is an exceptional player, as is their offensive line," Helfrich said after the game. "Their offensive line did a really nice job."

Ducks quarterback Marcus Mariota tries to escape Buckeyes defensive tackle Michael Bennett (53). *Ric Tapia | AP Photo*

OSU stopped the Ducks on fourth down with less than four minutes to play, taking over in Oregon territory. Elliott capped a short Buckeye drive with another touchdown for the final points of the game.

Elliott finished the season with 1,878 rushing yards, good for second-most in program history.

In addition to Elliott's third-straight game with 220 yards or more, Jones finished the night 16-of-23 on pass attempts for 242 yards and a touchdown with one interception. Jalin Marshall led the Buckeyes with five receptions while redshirt-junior wide receiver Corey Smith totaled 76 yards through the air.

Powell led OSU with nine total tackles while Washington and sophomore safety Vonn Bell each tallied sacks of Mariota.

Mariota finished the game with 333 passing yards and two touchdowns, while Byron Marshall tallied eight receptions for 169 yards and a score. OSU redshirt-freshman cornerback Eli Apple forced Oregon's only turnover with an interception of Mariota on the game's final play.

The 14 wins are tied for the most in OSU history, and the 15 games played by both teams marks the most by any program in a single season.∎

BOX SCORE

	1	2	3	4	T
Oregon #2	7	3	10	0	20
Ohio State #4	14	7	7	14	42

SCORING SUMMARY

FIRST QUARTER
ORE   TD   12:21   Keanon Lowe 7 Yd pass from Marcus Mariota (Aidan Schneider Kick)
Drive info: 11 plays, 75 yds in 2:39
OSU   TD   4:36   Ezekiel Elliott 33 Yd Run (Sean Nuernberger Kick)
Drive info: 10 plays, 97 yds in 3:16
OSU   TD   1:08   Nick Vannett 1 Yd pass from Cardale Jones (Sean Nuernberger Kick)
Drive info: 4 plays, 46 yds in 1:27

SECOND QUARTER
OSU   TD   4:49   Cardale Jones 1 Yd Run (Sean Nuernberger Kick)
Drive info: 6 plays, 49 yds in 2:16
ORE   FG   0:48   Aidan Schneider 26 Yd Field Goal
Drive info: 12 plays, 66 yds in 4:01

THIRD QUARTER
ORE   TD   11:23   Byron Marshall 70 Yd pass from Marcus Mariota (Aidan Schneider Kick)
Drive info: 1 plays, 70 yds in 0:10
ORE   FG   6:39   Aidan Schneider 23 Yd Field Goal
Drive info: 6 plays, 17 yds in 1:42
OSU   TD   0:00   Ezekiel Elliott 9 Yd Run (Sean Nuernberger Kick)
Drive info: 12 plays, 75 yds in 6:39

FOURTH QUARTER
OSU   TD   9:44   Ezekiel Elliott 2 Yd Run (Sean Nuernberger Kick)
Drive info: 9 plays, 76 yds in 4:13
OSU   TD   0:28   Ezekiel Elliott 1 Yd Run (Sean Nuernberger Kick)
Drive info: 5 plays, 14 yds in 2:17

Ohio State head coach Urban Meyer celebrates after holding Oregon on a fourth down play during the second half. With the win over the Ducks, Meyer joins Alabama's Nick Saban as the only coaches to win a national championship at two schools. *Brandon Wade | AP Photo*

Cardale Jones is all smiles after helping the Buckeyes beat Oregon for the school's 8th National Championship.
David J. Phillip | AP Photo

Offensive Player of the Game Ezekiel Elliott kisses the championship trophy. *LM Otero | AP Photo*

Ohio State's Taylor Decker, (68) and Jeff Heuerman (5) celebrate with their teammates. *David J. Phillip | AP Photo*

An Ohio State fan lets everyone know the Buckeyes just won their 8th National Championship.
LM Otero | AP Photo